The Child Worshipers

THE

Child

Worshipers

MARTHA WEINMAN LEAR

Crown Publishers, Inc.

New York

Parts of the chapters "In Health," "In Style," and "In Business" first appeared in The New York Times Magazine. Copyright 1960, 1961 by The New York Times Co. Reprinted by permission.

In the chapter "In Style," the poem "Triolet on a Flat Failure" is used by permission of the author, Margaret Fishback Antolini.

In the chapter "At the Summit," material quoted from Boris M. Levinson's "The Intellectually Exceptional Child: Part II, The Intellectually Gifted Child" (Yeshiva Education, IV:1, 1961) is used by permission of Dr. Levinson.

Library of Congress Catalog Card Number: 63-12069

Printed in the United States of America

Third Printing, December, 1963

FOR KENIA

And in joyous memory of Joe

THE CHILD WORSHIPERS

The Child Worshipers

INTRODUCTION

It has been called, variously, a pediocracy, a filiarchy or, in the stern sociological view, a filio-centric way of life. Hordes of experts and quasi experts have gone into the field to study the phenomenon, and have emerged with the same mournful intelligence: We are living, like it or not—and the fact that we created it does not necessarily mean we like it—in a child-centered society. Having passed more or less unscathed through the bittersweet epoch of Life With Father, and having survived, somehow, the rigors of Momism, we are come upon a time when the child carries the ball. It is a sort of historical triple pass—from Poppa to Momma to Junior—and Junior, at the moment, is out in front and running free. Or so they say.

But parents have, after all, been in that particular bind for years. As far back as 1831, Mrs. Trollope, taking one of her better potshots, chidingly noted: "I have conversed with many American ladies on the total want of discipline and subjection which I observed universally among children of all ages, and I never found any who did not both acknowledge and deplore the truth of the remark. In the state of Ohio, they have a law . . . that if a father strike his son he shall pay a fine of ten dollars for every such offence. I was told by a gentleman of Cincinnati, that he had seen this fine inflicted there, at the requisition of a boy of twelve years of age, whose father, he proved, had struck him for lying. Such a law, they say, generates a spirit of freedom. What else may it generate?"

Thus we have the comfort, whatever its worth, of a certain cultural continuity. But whereas Mrs. Trollope and her fellow critics saw the American child as merely undisciplined, over-indulged, and otherwise beastly, today's chroniclers have added a new dimension to the same old lament: The child, they say, is in control.

And, indeed, a preponderance of research suggests that children do control the pattern of family life to an awesome degree. Whole communities are geared largely to their needs. They dominate adult conversation—especially in their absence. Gone are the halcyon days when mothers sat at one end of the room talking about natural childbirth and fathers stood at the other talking turkey. Today they mingle, and they talk—from the heart—about how tough it is to get into a good nursery school.

Children determine, more often than not, where the family will live. They determine what kind of home it will rent or buy; how it will spend its leisure hours; whom it will befriend; when and where it will vacation; what car it will drive; what foods it will eat, and how it will spend its income upon the myriad educational, social, and cultural activities deemed essential to the burgeoning psyche. And their parents—hounded by ghosts of Freud, harassed by bevies of experts, painfully eager to do the right thing by their offspring, to understand him, to relate to him in Meaningful Ways, to win his love, ward off his traumas, and give him every known advantage and some totally unknown beyond our national borders— these parents, almost inevitably, have pushed the child stage center, casting him in a role he never asked to play but which he has learned to play right well.

But is he really running the show? Unlikely. The current mode is to speak, with much wringing of hands, of "child rule," "child tyrants," the "Grand Abdication" of parental authority. It is an expedient fiction, rendering parents helpless before a high command of pre-pubescent tots. The likelier fact is this: Baby is being used. He is a front-runner, groomed to show the world what hotshots his parents are.

Striving so passionately to be Good Parents—the ultimate accolade in these child-minded times—many mothers and fathers have turned parenthood into a painfully competitive sport. In an era when traditional status symbols can turn obsolescent overnight, they have discovered that social stature may still be gained by raising the best-dressed, -fed, -educated, -mannered, -medicated, -cultured, and -adjusted child on the block. If he looms discomfortingly large, it is only because they have done their job so well. Exploiting their child, they have created a turning worm, a faithless Galatea—a paragon of such power that he has become the exploiter, and they the victims of their own exploitation.

These are the parents we call the child worshipers. They are not, as we shall see, always permissive; for competitive parents are generally pediatric trend-followers and they know that permissiveness is a trifle passé nowadays. But they *are* self-conscious, self-doubting, and deeply immersed in the care and psychic feeding of children. Worshipers are compulsive parents. Their rallying cry, although they sometimes wish fervently they could stop shouting it, is "for the sake of the children"; and their goal, although they sometimes wish prayerfully they could forget it, is to be Good Parents in the eyes of the child psychiatrists, the child guidance experts, the Parents' Club membership, and, of course, the neighbors.

Are we talking about all parents? All children? Of course not. There are still plenty of parents who hold the reins taut, who are not afraid of being rejected by their offspring, who can whack misbehavers without feeling guilty, who can say "No" to fancy birthday parties and posh camps and social dancing lessons and organized play and high-fashion wardrobes and child-decorated homes and optional orthodontia and Mothers' Clubs and Ivy League hysteria—all of which we will take up in due time—without fear of traumatizing their young. And there are still plenty of children around who are suffering such quaint deprivations nicely, and may even survive. All American parents are not child worshipers any more than all American adults are joiners, or all American business is big, or all American families eat hot dogs. But we *are* a nation of joiners, of big business, of hot-dog eaters; and in this sense we are a nation of child worshipers.

Most parents exhibit some of the characteristics of the breed; relatively few exhibit all. This book will be concerned primarily with the true-blue, to-the-death child worshipers: with what they do, and how and why they do it. But it will occasionally take the broad, or national, view; for child worship is in some ways a national epidemic, and the fact that no one has made a statistical survey does not invalidate what is all too evident in almost any community in the land. Nor by community do we necessarily mean the suburb, which has had the finger pointed at it long enough. Child-happy people abound everywhere, as witness the racy dinner-party talk—"No, he's not a great science teacher, but he relates so well to the children"—that may be overheard in the dark, exotic heart of Manhattan.

Much that the child worshipers do is funny, although sometimes it hurts to laugh; much is exasperating, and some, particularly as it concerns manipulating children for social status, is appalling. Out of many illustrative possibilities, we have chosen to show the worshipers at work in ten specific areas of the child's social, academic, and cultural life. And because child worship is gamiest and goriest in the early years, we will confine ourselves to the span from infancy to puberty, by which time, presumably, the child is either a full-fledged status symbol or a teen-ager with other problems.

A final point: the multitudinous studies, in or out of depth, that have been made in the name of sociology hardly leave room for another, and this most emphatically is not another. The approach is reportorial: first, because journalism, not sociology, is this writer's profession; and secondly, because child worship is rather a new phenomenon and thus best uncovered through legwork. Hence the technique has been to go directly to the parent educators, the child psychiatrists, the pediatricians, the teachers, the I.Q. testers, the camp counselors, the toy makers, the box-top brokers, the dancing-school masters, the birthday-party coordinators—and, of course, to the child worshipers themselves. And because nobody personifies the spirit of child worship so clearly as the truly dedicated Good Mother, we will start with her.

M. W. L.

AT THE STARTING LINE

The Good Mother

She works at motherhood relentlessly, as others do at femininity or at golf. Various observers may question her methods, and various observers do, but none can fault her on effort, sincerity, or utter devotion to duty. Yet she is not, if the question be put to her, a child-centered woman; one rarely meets a child-centered woman, although one meets a good many women whose friends are all child-centered. And in a certain traditional sense her self-image is correct. She is not the Mom who has baby shoes cast in bronze, for example, or trots out pictures of the wee ones. That is not the Good Mother's style at all. Her child-centeredness is less a matter of adoration than of preoccupation. She is not busy doting on her children, but understanding them (educator Harold Taylor has commented feelingly on the plight of the contemporary child, all too well "understood") and doing what is *good* for them—including, when necessary, taking a hard line. Though she may incline toward the indulgent approach, she is aware of that "generation of monsters" for which Anna Freud has so graciously taken, in her father's name, some burden of responsibility, and tries to temper her own permissiveness. Thus it is that she doesn't think of herself as child-centered. She is determined, consciously determined, *not* to be child-centered. Rather like the fellow determined not to think of hippopotami.

"Not me!" she may say, as one did recently. "My kids are disciplined. Discipline is good for children. All the experts say so." Or: "My husband and I don't want everything to be focused on the kids. We are very conscious of the danger. We discuss it all the time." If she is really sharp she understands the mechanism fully. One says, "My friends and I used to talk children, children, children constantly. Now we lean over backward not to. I think we have become a little frightened by our preoccupation with children."

Most of her tensions, her anxieties, her gratifications, and her aspirations center on the children. The interpretations and misinterpretations of Freud that have sifted down through the years have left her with the conviction that if a first-rate acorn blossoms into a third-rate oak, it is nobody's fault but her own; and this, of course, means that guilt is forever tapping her on the shoulder. The time and energy she devotes to becoming a better mother, a less protective mother, a less indulgent mother, a less self-conscious mother, a *less involved* mother, make her possibly one of the most supremely involved mothers of all time. She is, in short, pre-eminently the professional mother—a phrase applied by Dr. Florence Kluckhohn of Harvard to describe the woman who makes motherhood the super-duper, full-time career. Witness:

"I come home from a hard day's work. I say, 'What's

new?' She says, 'What could be new out here?' I say, 'Why don't you get a job?' She says, 'I can't. The kids need me.' I say, 'Why don't we move back to the city?' She says, 'We can't. The kids need fresh air.' I say, 'Great. They've got you and they've got fresh air. You're all set.' She says, 'Thanks a lot.' "

"I was too busy to take the baby out one day, and I felt I had failed him. I mentioned it to the pediatrician and he said, 'Believe me, Mrs. T., by the time he is married he'll have forgotten all about it.' I had to laugh at myself, but I *did* feel better."

"My friend had a fight with her husband in front of their five-year-old daughter. She's very psychiatry-minded, and she's been worried sick about its effect on the child. That kind of thinking is contagious. Now I'm careful, too. And even if I'm saying to my husband 'You bastard,' which our eight-month-old wouldn't understand anyway, I say it softly and with a smile on my face."

"My son was in bed with a cold. I had lots of things to do and I felt guilty being out all day while he was cooped up in the apartment with just the cleaning woman for company. So I canceled my lunch date and zipped through my beauty parlor appointment and grabbed a cab home and rushed into his room and said, 'Okay, I'm ready now. What will we play?' And he said, 'I don't know about you, Mom, but I have homework. Can't you find something to do?' "

Good mothers, all. Some seem to think they have some native habitat; they have none. A. C. Spectorsky found them in Exurbia, and wrote in his celebrated tract on that outpost:

"The exurbs and all exurban life are primarily centered around the children. A couple may have had all sorts of bemused reasons for moving so far from the city, but the wife had one compelling one: her children are out of the city in the country, away from expensive private schools or inferior public schools, with plenty of children just like themselves for companionship. It is for these pleasant surroundings and for the children that the exurban wife will endure the very real discomforts of her life. . . ."

William H. Whyte, Jr., found them in suburbia—specifically, Park Forest, Illinois—and wrote in *The Organization Man:* "It begins with the children. There are so many of them and they are so dictatorial in effect that a term like *filiarchy* would not be entirely facetious. . . ."

Sidonie Gruenberg, long one of the lights of the parent education movement, has said: "They [the suburban mothers] find no outlets for their talents and energies and they tend to focus all their efforts upon their children. . . ."

But a noted big-city educator comments: "In the city it's the same damn thing, but in another suit of clothes. The concentration on the kids may be more psychological than physical, but it is still total."

Certainly the child-rearing experts are as busy in the city as anywhere else, soothing the Good Mother's troubled soul. The park benches are weighty with women eying the sandpile and speaking of sex education. The P.T.A. battalions are large, the pediatricians are bushed, the parent groups proliferate. All of parent education, in fact, flourishes like a rain forest, needing only the Good Mother for its nurture. For she is an exceedingly cerebral parent, who is much given to psychiatric ponderings and theoretical discussions of her role; motherhood does not, except in its biological sense, seem to come naturally to her. "In other cultures," a sociologist has commented, "it would be ludicrous to think of 'parent education.' They teach each other, mother to daughter. Here it would be ludicrous to think how we would function *without* parent education."

She may belong to a Parent Group or, a short hop down the socioeconomic ladder, a Mothers' Club. She may attend lectures. She may simply browse periodically through the plentiful pickings in books (more than four hundred hardcover parent-education books are published yearly), magazines, and newspaper columns. But she knows what the experts are saying and she strives heroically to keep her head in the face of their onslaughts of conflicting advice.

Parent educators are essentially anti-expert experts. They aim, as one has put it, "to teach mothers to relax more, to throw away the rule books and act natural with their youngsters, be spontaneous." This altogether commendable goal poses a certain dilemma for the Good Mother, understandably rattled in the face of so many people teaching her how to be spontaneous. Further, her dilemma is self-perpetuating: the more outside help she gets in pursuit of her own instinctual knowledge, the more outside help she seems to need. In effect: Tell me what my inner voice is saying.

And they do. No self-respecting newspaper is without a parent education column nowadays, even though the content can hardly help tracking ground that has been deeply trodden in other media. The women's magazines, understandably, are absorbed with parent-child problems ("How Well Are You Raising Your Children?" "How Often Do You Insult Your Child?"—and from a dissident, "Who Says Children Are Human?" Occasionally they are faintly antagonistic—"Parents Have Rights, Too" "So I'm *Not* a Perfect Parent!"—and often they are in gross disharmony. Not long ago, while two coverlines proclaimed "Play Ball with Your

Kids!" and "Have Fun with Your Son!", two others demurred in heavy type: "Who Needs a Parent Pal?" and "Leave Your Kids Alone!") The subject saturates the "family" magazines and even the newsweeklies ("Are We Trapped in a Child-Centered World?" asked *Newsweek* breathlessly, and then, surveying the sorely maligned suburbs, the junior social whirls, the myriad parent organizations, the army of critical experts, it stoutly answered its own question: "Perhaps never before have adults worked so hard at the function of making the family unit productive and balanced. Most U.S. parents are not child-centered. They are family-centered. . . .")

But it is the parent group (a semantic nicety; relatively few fathers participate) that looms largest in parent education today. As a toiler in these fertile vineyards says, "Spock can tell mothers what to do in a given situation, but he can't give them a friendly ear or a pat on the back when they're feeling low. A parent group can."

Loosely defined, a parent group is any assemblage of parents that meets regularly for the purpose of talking about children. P.T.A.'s are, of course, a prime example, but parent groups also may be, and are, affiliated with churches, canasta clubs, and research centers. Such trail-blazers as the Child Study Association and the League for Parent Education operate vast networks of parent-group units. They invite mothers to form their own neighborhood groups, help them organize, outline their programs, give them literature, and even supply them, upon request, with trained group leaders.

It is not, of course, every Good Mother's cup of tea. For example, it is not for the sophisticate who laughs with merry self-deprecation ("My God, listen to me. Isn't it *nauseating?*") whenever she find herself talking about children. Such a mother tends to consider the parent-group approach déclassé, and wouldn't be caught dead bringing her problems to a group meeting, although she may not mind bringing them to a psychiatrist. But for less chic souls parent-group participation is wonderfully therapeutic.

What do members talk about? An intrepid lady psychologist who shepherds several mothers' clubs through their monthly meetings once tried to list all the topics she had covered in the course of a year, and came up with no fewer than 103. Among them: Sex Information; Danger of Too Much Sex Information; The Child's Need for Authority; The Bossy Toddler; Inflexible Mother Versus Aggressive Child; Asserting One's Own Rights With Children; and Toughening Up Children—by what means, one hardly dare ask. "Recently," she says, "we have been talking a lot about leadership. Since Kennedy and the astronauts, every mother wants her child to be a leader. And 'values'—what should they be and how should you impart them to your children?"

Despite such metaphysical forays, parent-groupers generally are concerned with more practical stuff. "Actually," says the lady psychologist, "they'll listen to anything as long as it's supporting. Reassurance—that's what they want."

And reassurance is what they get. An instance: the monthly meeting of a large, hyper-active parents' group in a middling-size northern Connecticut community. The speaker, billed as "writer and lecturer," is making her third annual appearance—a proven favorite. The subject: Do You Communicate With Your Child?

"I know this will be a treat for you all," begins the chairlady. "And after you hear our speaker, you will end up wondering what's the matter with you—not with your child. We as parents have got to try to reach our children, and I am sure she will help us to do so."

The guest opens on a note generally favored by her ilk: "This is a difficult time in which to bring up children, and

we are all seeking desperately for the answers. Perhaps together, we shall be able to find a few of them.

"Now, then. Why did you come tonight? Because you're
ignorant." She pauses as the crowd sighs mournfully, then
continues with a chipper smile. "But it's a *dynamic* ignorance,
not a static ignorance." The audience, breathing easier,
chuckles back at her.

The speaker then moves trippingly, painlessly, through the
pocked ground of parental problems, touching here upon
bedtime belligerence, there upon table manners. So grateful
is the audience to learn that these are, as she keeps stressing,
common experiences, that its spirits grow until by the time
she broaches the issue of mopping up after sloppy children
the lecture hall is aglow with neighborly cheer. The listeners
nod happily when she speaks of temper tantrums, laugh with
sympathetic clubbiness when she rings in sibling rivalry, and
grow positively giddy with gratitude, relief, and mutual good
will when she manages to tiptoe lightly over petty thievery
("Let's face it, people—*every* child goes through that
period").

With feeling thus running warm and high, she winds up
on a note of splendid conviction, more than compensating
her listeners for that ignorance, albeit dynamic, of which
she had earlier accused them. "And what do we do about these
problems?" she says. "Well, I wouldn't presume to tell you.
You all have your own answers. But isn't it *good* to know that
we're all in the same boat?" The audience, solidly hers now,
applauds roundly, and it is time for questions.

"It's always the same thing," she said later, looking
morosely into a third cup of coffee. "The same questions,
the same problems. I don't even have to listen. If I just nod
and say, 'Oh, you poor thing,' they beam.

"What I get fed up with is the awful, pious self-consciousness of these women who are so determinedly being 'good' mothers. They are such worriers. You can't *imagine* what worriers they are."

One would hope such yeomanlike expenditure of work and worry is good for the Good Mother's children. But how good is it for her? On this score she herself may feel a certain ambivalence, which a psychiatrist pinpoints thusly: "A patient tells me, 'It's dull being with kids, kids, kids. I wish I could escape.' But if *you* tell *her* it's dull being with kids, kids, kids, you'd better duck."

One who didn't duck is writer and critic Marya Mannes, and in this regard her experience is noteworthy. Miss Mannes, a courageous thinker, wrote an article for *The New York Times Magazine* a while back, which held in part that the woman who wants to apply her intelligence to the creation of more than children ought to have society's blessing, and more power to her. She further suggested that a public school nursery system, such as functions in Britain, Sweden, Denmark, and elsewhere, might be a fine innovation here. This engendered a number of seismographic reactions via reader mail, whose prevailing sentiment seemed to be that Miss Mannes was un-American and ought to be sent back to wherever she came from, which happens to be New York.

"You would have thought," she recalls, still a trifle shaken, "that I had struck at the core of motherhood. Some of the letters were vicious. The anger of these women is a remarkable thing.

"I think my comment about the day nurseries was what got them maddest. They operate on the assumption that a mother has *got* to be with her children twenty-four hours a day. They resent the woman who goes to work simply because she wants to. They have thought themselves into a box of mothering, and when they encounter someone who has thought herself out of it they feel gypped, and they are furious." (The only nastier mail she ever received, Miss Mannes adds, was from abstract artists—another cause, another conflict.)

A free-lance writer, Gael Greene, had a similarly trying experience following the publication of an article. But then, Miss Greene really went too far: the piece was called "A Vote Against Motherhood," and it heaped insult upon injury by appearing in *The Saturday Evening Post.* Miss Greene made clear that it was only *her* vote, and that she wasn't proselytizing. Nonetheless, the injured parties numbered into the several thousands. While many seemed genuinely to pity her ("Seeing your children grow into happy, useful people— graduating from the best colleges on the honor roll—producing grandchildren who put their arms around you to tell you they love you . . . This will never be your privilege"), others were enraged. Readers called her all manner of names, such as a spoiled and selfish woman, a shriveled and stunted personality, even "judging from your horrible photograph . . . a worn-out prostitute."

The pertinent point here is not Miss Greene's opinion of motherhood, which is a very private matter, or Miss Mannes' opinion of professional motherhood, which is a very public matter, but the vitriolic reaction they generated. Why the intensity of these readers?

"Because motherhood is their *raison d'être,*" says the director of a noted family counseling service. "You take that away, and what have they got left?

"Mothers used to just go about their business. Now they worry about how to 'fulfill' themselves—and they have no way except through the kids, so they throw themselves into the job with great energy. At the same time they don't really find it too fulfilling, and this makes them twice as energetic and twice as defensive when they are challenged.

"Many of these gals have gone to college, they're smart, they're trained for something more than the daily duties of motherhood. Yet they find themselves with motherhood as their career, and the only way they can show how sharp they are is *as mothers*. So they say, 'Okay, then, I'll be the best damn mother you ever saw.' "

Thus kicking off the herculean rivalry. For many child worshipers—those professional mothers of Dr. Kluckhohn's phrase—motherhood is indeed a career, as tough and competitive as any other. "Such women," says Dr. Kluckhohn, "are in effect telling their children, 'I hate to cook and clean and be just a housewife. I am doing it for you, and so you owe me an obligation.' " The obligation? To succeed.

Enter, beaming (and why wouldn't he be? He's got the best damn mother you ever saw), the status-symbol child. What does his mother *really* want? Why, whatever is best for him; nothing new there—parents have always wanted the best for their children. But at some point, for some mothers, the motives have gotten muddled. Whoever can raise the best-of-breed gets to wear the ribbon, and at this juncture it is often hard to tell which is uppermost in their minds— the welfare of the child or the sporting of the ribbon.

The results are twofold. The first is the hard manipulation of children, a subject about which experts lately have been exchanging a lot of talk, all of it serious. Educators and medical people have been deeply concerned by the increased incidence of colitis and ulcers in elementary schoolers as a product of parental pressures.

The other result gets much less attention, which is a pity; it is a simply perfect boomerang. "Our children," says a parent educator, "are becoming victims of parental competition." Victims! Behold this *pauvre petit:* ruthlessly groomed for the best schools, subjected to the fanciest birthday parties, burdened by the most expensive (educational) toys, the chicest clothes . . . Is Baby being used? Yes indeed, in many cases. Is he being manipulated toward his own eventual ruination? Possibly so. But glory, glory, what a helluva way to die!

Fortunately, the competitive parent often does a good job in spite of herself. As a school psychiatrist says: "Suppose a kid gets smothered in cultural activities so his mother will have an edge on the neighbors. Her motives are wrong, but there's nothing wrong with culture.

"Or look at this nursery school business. Some mothers take fiendish delight in getting their kids into nursery school very early. The mother may say she is doing it because the kid has nobody to play with at home. We *know* it is also because she wants him to have a jump on the other kids when he gets into kindergarten. She also wants to keep up with her friends, who are sending *their* kids to nursery school. But the child isn't getting a bad deal—unless, of course, he hates nursery school. I'd even say he has it pretty good. He's being provided with playmates."

The mechanism appears in countless guises:

A publisher of encyclopedias beams an advertisement at parents. An encyclopedia assuredly will do a child no harm, but note the sales pitch: "How will they measure up against the kids next door? Uncomfortable as the idea is, this is the time to face it. Everyone wants more for his children. And your children will have to compete just as *you're* competing now in the adult world. . . ."

A psychologist smiles a puzzled, not unhappy smile. "I get paid a tidy sum by a toy manufacturer to age-grade toys," he says. "Really, I think it's a waste of his money, although [smile broadening] let's not tell anyone about it. A mother doesn't buy the toys that are *average*. You always find the five-year-old playing with toys that are age-graded for seven-year-olds, which gives his mama something to talk about at the bridge table."

Similarly, says a school psychiatrist, "You get the three-year-old whose mother mentions nonchalantly that he likes to play *constructively*. And the two-year-old who can do the calypso. And when they get down to ages where they can't *do* anything, you switch to what they eat. 'The four-month-old down the block is eating chopped meat—why can't mine?' This is the kind of thing that drives pediatricians out of their minds." Or at least out of pediatrics, as will be seen shortly.

The parent who competes through her children is a subject this psychiatrist has sunk his teeth into before many a parent group; and the only reason he has escaped intact, he says, is because every mother is privately convinced he is talking about every member of the audience except herself. "They are always horrified, of course. They say, 'Is this true? Let's do a statistical survey.' Naturally that wouldn't prove a thing because these competitive motives are largely unconscious. But the competition is just as deadly even if we can't document it."

With what result? "Well, it reminds me of the woman who is a slave to all her work-saving gadgets. When you start using children to satisfy your own competitive drives, you become very dependent on them. They may end up in control."

And Margaret Mead has put the matter in spanking good style: "There is the question of whether we are going to sit children at the table in high chairs, thus implying their place with the family, or sit on the floor with them. We used to put them in high chairs, but then many of us began sitting on the floor."

There many might have remained—except that the Good

Mother, her spiritual backside tiring perhaps, rebelled. She began seeking a seating arrangement that would allow her to be comfortable as well as Good, and indications are that she may have found it. What pointed the way, oddly enough, was the very instrument that once nearly brought her to her Götterdämmerung: Togetherness.

It was born, as the world knows all too well, in the front offices of *McCall's* magazine in 1954, and lived the high life while it lasted. It won a Freedoms Foundation Award. It won a special citation from the Gold Star Mothers. Senator Hubert Humphrey read a tribute to it on the Senate floor. California Congressman Craig Homer read a tribute to it on the House floor, which found posterity in the *Congressional Record.* The United States Post Office issued a stamp called "The American Woman," bearing a picture of a mother and child. David Riesman called it "a fine ideal."

John Mason Brown, on the other hand, called it "a kind of diabetic quality of sugar in the blood." Philip Wylie said, "To Hell with Togetherness." Cartoonists were merciless. Two memorable examples: Charles Addams' Siamese twins poring over a copy of *McCall's;* a family of robbers hastily exiting from a bank, the caption reading: "There's real Togetherness for you." Li'l Abner slapped down his son for demanding a private comb. "Th' family whut combs together stays together!"

Sticks and stones. Togetherness took them in its mighty stride. It had become, as *McCall's* pointed out, "the word that has captured America . . . a new word for a new pattern of living."

This was the spirit, and thousands saluted it. A vice-president of Foote, Cone and Belding, an advertising agency, saluted it: "Togetherness is more than just a big word. It is a big *concept.* Don't just look for it in the dictionary. The place to find it is in the human heart."

An official of the KLM Royal Dutch Airlines saluted it: *"McCall's* 'Togetherness' campaign opens the door to richer family relationships, and family travel fulfills the goal of unity toward which all families head."

A perfume manufacturer, Lentheric, saluted it: "Togetherness is most certainly reflected in the increased fragrance buying habits of today's American women. We find them buying more fragrances for every member of the family, as well as for themselves."

An executive of Jackson China saluted it: "Togetherness means being together and enjoying things together . . . including mealtimes. Today, we see more Togetherness in the purchase of china. Both wife and husband make the selection for lasting Togetherness."

A vice-president of U.S. Plywood saluted it: "Here in our showroom it's women, women, women . . . and the men agreeing with them. The concept of Togetherness is really showing up in our industry." Toymakers, Inc., saluted it; The U.S. Trunk Co., Inc., saluted it; Exquisite Form Brassiere, Inc., saluted it (*"McCall's* has created . . . an ideal setting for the sales message of a product which by enhancing female beauty fosters family Togetherness"); and the United Fruit Company saluted it: "Bananas are a family food enjoyed through life. In fact, bananas are often the first solid food in an infant's diet. The new trend in family living termed Togetherness . . . allows more people more opportunities to enjoy this fabulous fruit."

The bloom lasted for more than five years, and in the end it was the magazine itself that called it quits. An editor says: "We decided to go back to being a woman's magazine for women. Our new view was to bring beauty back into life instead of pushing a grim determination to be together."

By then *McCall's* wasn't the only one that yearned to cry uncle. *"Must* we be together all the time?" a mother asked dolefully in a parent-education column. "I would like some apartness now and then, but I want to do what is good for the family. . . ."

Were the two irreconcilable? Not at all. Out of this very conflict has emerged a new concept, a new manner of mothering, whose possibilities we have only begun to explore. It is Togetherness modified by Apartheid. Basically, it consists in doing the best and the most for one's children, but doing it by proxy—thus leaving the mother free of guilt and free of child. The system works well in the field of organized play—community centers, recreation programs, day camps— all with their built-in baby sitters. The technique even embraces family vacations, which once were the triumph of force-fed Togetherness but now may be arranged so as to give parents and children minimal exposure to each other.

"The women in this town don't do everything they do for their kids because they believe in it or because the kids enjoy it," says an elementary school principal, "but because they feel they should. Most of the things they have their children doing are what the kids are sent to do with *other* parents, such as athletic coaches and Scout leaders."

"Children here are talked about a great deal," says a European psychiatrist currently scrutinizing the local scene. "It is my impression that they are more talked about than cared for. The talk comes out of guilt, and the guilt comes out of neglect. While the youngsters are kept unnecessarily busy they do not have to be tended by parents. And meanwhile the parents can point to all they are doing for their children.

"I think this neglect is in part a reaction to certain social pressures—the pressure of Togetherness, for example, which when it was popular became an obligation. Women got fed up with it. In other countries—Russia, most assuredly [oh, harsh words]—parents practice Togetherness much more than you preach it here. I mean in the good, natural sense—doing things with children out of enjoyment rather than out of a sense of guilt or duty."

"This is a very devious form of neglect," says a native-born practitioner, speaking without the constraints of diplomacy. "In the early days of psychiatry every adult who was sick had been rejected by his mother. Today the mother deceives herself. She puts the kids out of the house, but she doesn't just throw them into the street. She delivers them to their friends' houses—which, incidentally, gives her something to complain about. When she goes shopping, she doesn't leave the poor babes home drying the dishes, she drops them off at the community center on her way downtown. Then she meets the girls and what do they talk about? Children. She is more involved with children than she ever was—but she has worked out a very sophisticated *modus vivendi.*

"There are two ways to reject a child," says our psychiatric man fretfully, "and today, heaven help us, one of them is socially acceptable."

AT HOME

The Children's Wing

Not quite speechless with indignation at the injustice of it all, the editor of a ladies' home-decorating magazine recently took up the cudgels. "We aren't the least bit certain that we would like being a child in this day and age," she wrote. "Our reason is simply that we just can't see ourselves fitting into the average house being built today. It seems to us that very few houses now are designed with children in mind."

To the gentlemen of the homebuilding business, this must come as a revelation. They haven't worried about the problem because they didn't know it existed, the situation as they see it being that very few houses are designed with anything *but* children in mind. As summed up by one of the largest homebuilders on the East Coast:

"In the good old days, architects directed the planning

of houses. Now . . ."—a pained squint, a deep sigh—"children do."

In those clear, balmy days of which he spoke, people who lived in houses generally lived in rooms. Children lived in bedrooms, ate in dining rooms, played in playrooms, were told to keep out of living rooms and sometimes, exotic as the notion may now seem, even out of kitchens.

Then, with a creative shattering of walls, doors, and other such amenities, in came the open-floor plan, and soon there were no rooms left to keep out of. In the beginning, open-floor dwelling was custom dwelling, and it was taken up by that affluent segment of society which, being avant-garde about most other matters, was avant-garde about its children as well. Indeed, the open-floor plan and progressive parenthood seemed tailormade for each other, neither cottoning to such senile concepts as children knowing their place. The children's place was everyplace; in the open-plan home they could be isolated behind no barrier heavier than a shoji screen —a weak-kneed notion of apartheid at best—or confined in the bathroom, which, if one exempts the front and back doors, often boasted the last honest door of its era. And so everybody traveled together, in steerage as it were, in the hold of a $50,000 home.

From that point on, there seems to be a curious parallel between what happened in the fields of child development and homebuilding. When Permissiveness, strictly a pace-setting concept through the Thirties and well into the Forties, start gaining mass appeal, the open-floor plan went into mass production. Particularly in the postwar years, with the baby rate booming and veterans stampeding for cheap housing spacious enough to accommodate the boom, the open-floor design was an ideal solution for making small houses look bigger than they were.

By the mid-1950's, open-floor living and permissive child-raising had become so popularized that the trend-setters were tiring of both. And today, paralleling a cautious swing back to Discipline among parents who once were no-holds-barred permissive, we find a marked retreat in expensive home-building circles from the architectural Togetherness of the open-floor plan. "In the past two years," says the editor of a slick home-decorating publication, "I don't think we have printed a single open-floor-plan house. In the custom range you can't give them away."

The fashion now, she explains, is to "build the children away from" the adults. "In progressive architectural circles today the theory is that children are neither to be seen nor heard. The 'children's wing' is a very strong trend. It is kept apart from the master suite by a living area—the farther apart, the better. Almost every house we've shown recently has had a separate wing for the kiddies."

Does this development, then, reflect current child-raising theories? "Oh, absolutely. Permissiveness brought the child into the open; Discipline is sending him back to his own room. Now the separate-wing type of house is sifting down to the mass-production level, too, as people there are catching up with the new child-raising ideas."

To clinch the matter, other observers in the field relay the sobering news that the family room—prime symbol of the soul and spirit of its time—has had it, at least in homes that bear the kingpin decorators' stamp of approval. There are now *two* family rooms: one for the children and one for the older folks.

Even the most persistent disciples of open-floor living bow to the inevitable. "Nowadays," says a spokesman for Tech-built, Inc., a leading designer of open-floor-plan homes, "separation of the master suite is often wanted. Ideally, the house plan should be divided so that there is an outdoor area for adults as well as a separate one for children."

Remember the all-in-one patio?

"At all the housing conferences I've attended recently," says Herman York, a Long Island architect and designer of the three original models for the Long Island Levittown, "women strongly indicate that they have a yen for privacy. The kitchen–family area is the only area they want open-plan. I think all-in-one living fell flat on its face. We're looking for apartness now . . . we're hungering for it."

Does the spectacle of consigning the young to wings of their own signify that family life is growing less child-centered? Not at all.

There is, first, the very fact of buying a house. "Under the guise of 'doing it for the kids,' " says Stanley Shaftel, an architect and no man to beat about those dear-bought bushes that landscape the child-centered home, "parents buy themselves into a financial sewer. They need to have indoor and outdoor play areas because of the kids. A barbecue pit because of the kids . . . a pool because of the kids . . . Ridiculous! Who needs it? Not the kids. They might rather be living in a barn. They become the decisive factor in how the family will live because the parents make them that way."

Mr. Shaftel is against private ownership of houses, a quaint notion for a homebuilder. He believes houses should be run as public corporations, with the tenants holding stock. "The disadvantages in owning a house are enormous," he says feelingly. "Taxation, capital investment, maintenance, home improvements, loss of opportunity because of the anchor, not to mention the fact that in one's own home there is—there *must* be—a complete devotion to janitorial services.

"You know what one builder told me? He said, 'I've put in my years of mowing the lawn. Now that the kids are grown

I'm going back to the city. If I'm going to be a janitor, let me be a *real* janitor.' "

Those who live in houses "because of the kids" also are apt to pick their locations "because of the kids." Thus one builder has noted that when people are building or buying houses, the first question they ask is about the tax rate; the second, except when it is the first, is about the schools. "Once I got this couple looking at a house of mine out in Jersey. They're nuts about the place. The wife tells me, 'You know, we've been house-hunting for six months, and this is the only nice place we've seen that's in our budget. It is divine.' 'So buy it,' I say. They give me a deposit and they leave and this wife is so happy she's got tears in her eyes. And the next day the husband calls me up and boy, is he embarrassed. They can't take the house, he says. Why not? The school. His wife heard through a friend of a friend that the school is not so hot. It's not progressive enough, she says."

The builder, obviously a man of philosophical bent, shrugs one well-tailored shoulder. "I should care," he says. "I got the deposit."

Locations also may be chosen to enable children to keep up—or catch up—with the junior Joneses. Their parents may prefer the bracing rigidity of city pavements, or some simple spot where the old gang dwells, but nonetheless they go into an area where the children can, hopefully, cultivate the right friends—and get right out again when they find they cannot support their offspring in the plush style local etiquette demands. Ergo, this builder says, the brisk turnover in some of the fancier suburban neighborhoods.

There is then what one interior designer has called "the private bedroom syndrome." "We used to have trundle beds, two or three of us in a room, and it was plenty good enough. Now there's got to be a private room for each child." ("It is

a *maturing* experience. Having a room of their own gives
them a sense of the dignity of the individual"—a mother.)
And from the private bedroom it is only a short, logical hop
to the family room, heart and hearth of the child-centered
home.

While the precise date is unknown, the family room seems
to have come along some twelve years ago to replace the
pre-war cellar playroom. A good many architects take credit
for it. One of the editors at *House and Home* says that he and
his colleagues first stumbled upon it in 1951, in Oklahoma,
where a builder had finished a garage as a play area. Not
knowing what he wrought for the future—had he known,
he might have reconsidered—he called it a "family room."
Later planners adapted the family-room idea to the main
house, as being exquisitely in keeping with the then-flowering
Togetherness, and the boom was on.

Today, a housing expert estimates, 65 per cent of all
homes built in the United States have a family room or
reasonable facsimile. Even the elite who have moved on—
or back—to the house of many walls have feared to desert
the family concept. Rather have they expanded it, as noted
earlier, into junior and senior family rooms, thus providing
an eloquent commentary upon the current view of Togetherness
in custom classes.

One builder says that for the past half-dozen years the
planning of houses has centered about the family-room area.
Typically, there is a general kitchen–family room, open-
plan, according to the main line of thinking now, even if
the rest of the house is not. The area often also includes a
"mud room," usually located near the back door and described as an enclosure wherein the young man may be
decontaminated before going on to the main part of the house.

"You can merchandise the hell out of the mud-room area,"

he says. "It is one of the big selling points, like a lavatory with fancy sink counter, that you can exaggerate out of proportion to its importance. Give 'em a mud room and cut down somewhere else, and they won't even notice.

"In upstate New York we had one model of a house that was selling reasonably well. So we called some of the women in the development together for a conference [a common gimmick among builders, and dear to many homemakers] to see how the model could be improved even further before we built more of them. You know what they wanted most that this house lacked? A lavatory at the rear entrance, adjacent to the mud room, for the kids' use. We upped the price a bit and included the lavatory, and the house sold like crazy."

Worth the extra cost? Every bit of it, apparently. That extra area keeps the children from tracking dirt through the rest of the house, and thus lightens the mother's workload. "The only alternative," the builder suggests, "would be to teach the kids to be tidy, but I guess that's a pretty old-fashioned idea."

Thanks to the architecture of the child-centered home, the mother's place is in the kitchen more emphatically than ever. Note the terminology:

In a group of award-winning houses in California, the kitchen is called the "living kitchen." "I had the horrors," says Ada Louise Huxtable, architectural critic for *The New York Times,* after perusing these triumphs of planning. "The kitchen was the main room. It was the room people ate in, even with guests. There was no escape from it. And these were the *award-winning houses.* They may call it a 'living kitchen,' but it's still a kitchen and the house is so wrapped around it that a woman has a hard time getting out."

Then there is the "pass-through"—that hole in the wall

engineered to facilitate the passing of dishes into the dining area or family room; not at all incidentally, it enables a mother to pass a glance through solid walls, the better to keep an eye on her young at all times.

This is part of what builders call the "control center" concept in kitchen planning. "When a woman starts designing a kitchen," says architect Shaftel, "she wants it near— the back yard, so she can watch the kids; the back door, so she can pop snacks into their mouths; a bathroom, so she can hose them down; an indoor play area, so she can hear them. She wants to keep them near her all the time, yet not underfoot. All this, of course, protects the parent from constant direct contact with the children, yet prevents her from feeling guilty about neglecting them."

It is from this small, albeit architecturally sound, empire— open to the family room, adjacent to the mud room, backed up to the back yard and fitted out with a pass-through—that the woman of the house reigns. And if her control center is now, indeed, the kitchen, she has only herself to blame; after all, she designed it that way.

Nor is child-centeredness built into the house simply to meet today's requirements. "A woman comes to me to design a house," an architect says wonderingly. "Her daughter is an infant in the crib. And what does this woman say when she looks at the plans? 'Where am I going to have the reception when my Susan gets married? You have to give me a bigger foyer for the reception.'" Or the mother, he says, may be worried about where the children will dance when they grow up. Give her an "area" where her three-year-old will one day be able to roll back the rugs and swing out with his friends; give her an "area" where her two-year-old will hold court at a Sweet Sixteen soirée; give her an "area" where she will one day, God and Cambridge willing, throw a graduation party for her son, the Harvard man, as yet unborn.

Builders, knowing where the bread is buttered, lavish it with jam. Many who specialize in small houses pinch on other features to provide the extra space for play areas. One architect tells of remodeling a house for a woman with five children, ranging in age from six to seventeen. She had decided to convert a small area off the kitchen into a snack and recreation spot for the children, and to build a spacious study and workroom for her husband, but in mid-renovation she switched schemes. "She said the new room was coming along so nicely that she had decided to give it to the kids, and to give her husband this tiny kitchen area. After all, she said, he'd only use it nights and weekends." (If Daddy was bitter, he had nothing on the disenchanted father who mused recently: "My wife tells me art is the most important accessory in rooms today. I'll say. Kids' crayon drawings hanging all over the house. I do a little Sunday painting myself. It's all in the attic. No wall space.")

Many builders, when they furnish model homes, put their hearts and hopes into the children's bedrooms. "They know that's where the ultimate appeal is," says one decorator. "A builder may skimp on the living-room décor, but in the kids' rooms he'll have fancy wallpaper and rugs shaped like clowns and lambs gamboling all over the place. And then a prospective customer will come along and look and say to her husband, 'Oh, isn't this room just right for Peter!' And the house is sold.

"Of course, not all builders do that. There are two theories of presenting a model house. One is, show it to the public furnished in mediocre fashion, the way it will probably end up, but don't go overboard. Otherwise the wife will say, 'Yes, it looks great with all this fancy decorating, but *we* could never have it looking like this.' The other theory is, decorate the house to the hilt, that's what sells it—and *really* take a flyer in the children's rooms."

Current developments in the home-decorating field indicate, in fact, that what the builder won't do for the child's room the child will do himself. Many decorators now make it standard practice to hold separate "consultations" with the children of clients ("Any child over seven," one says, compromising regretfully. "A younger one might not yet know exactly what he wants.")

Interviewing children is a largely painless gimmick that makes many clients feel they are getting more of their money's worth. It is done frequently enough to have given rise to a small but not insiginificant body of research on the subject, offered herewith for the enlightenment of those who somehow may have missed the news:

Small boys like modern furniture. They like blue and red and orange, in that order. They very seldom like green and purple, for reasons largely unknown, although it may be assumed that some thoroughgoing decorator is looking into it.

Small girls like period furniture. They like yellow, pink, white and green. They are extremely conscious, even when *very* small, of wanting to be feminine, and incline to fight royal blue to the death.

This intelligence comes by courtesy of a representative of Michael Greer, Inc., a New York interior decorating firm. The informant also notes the importance of *emotionally* functional décor for children, and cites one way parents can give a little girl a sense of security: by allotting her a spot of her own where she can serve tea to her dolls. This firm also is strong for separate television sets in the children's rooms, on grounds that the young should be able to entertain themselves. Such amenities may be more for the convenience of the parents than the children—but they boomerang. A recent report shows that sales of separate TV sets, record players, and telephones for children's rooms are on the rise in all price brackets. The folks say they buy the child his own television set so that the one in the family room can be theirs alone, but if he ends up with a set of his own they hardly can claim to have won the battle of the dial—it's not even a draw. Similarly, the child's private telephone: "Parents say they want private phones for the children so the kids won't be hogging the line all the time," says a telephone company lady. "Don't get me wrong—we approve of it. We *love* it. But in *my* house we solve the problem differently: we don't let the kids hog the line."

Many mothers will spend extraordinary sums of money decorating daughters' rooms ("I want a really feminine room for her; it will make her *feel* more feminine"). But the problem, an interior designer notes, is trying to keep up with their changing tastes. The little girl who wants pink today wants chartreuse (pale) tomorrow. "Fortunately," he points out, "most kids are wildly destructive and the mothers have a good excuse to replace the stuff."

Such shenanigans are not restricted to the moneyed. A member of the decorating department of Bloomingdale's in New York reports: "Parents will come into the store and spend what even I, as a decorator, think is a lot of money for kids—$300 for a bedspread and coverlet. These people are far from rich. Many of them are living in $125-a-month apartments, with modest decorating budgets, and the exorbitant things they buy are for four- and five-year-olds.

"Take the canopy bed. A while back, every little girl suddenly wanted a canopy bed. I had one, a big fancy job, on display in one of our branch stores. It was $160 without the bedding, and there was a four-month wait on delivery.

What a run on that bed!—and as far as I know, the girls for whom it was bought were all under ten. One woman didn't want to wait, so she bought a $380 model that could be delivered immediately. She used the child as a whip over her husband, as many women do. When he complained she said, 'You want to deprive your daughter of the best?' " (*She* used the *child?* Come, come, madam. Who ended up sleeping on the $380 bed?)

"Another customer was ready to buy her daughter a $500 model. I dissuaded her. This particular woman could afford it, yes; but I felt there was something almost indecent about that kind of expenditure on a small child."

"What we try to do," says a member of one sophisticated home-decorating outfit, "is to create a room that the child will be able to grow in." (A familiar euphemism for "expensive.") "How much parents invest in the children's rooms depends on whether a woman has her home decorated to show off or to please her family." Overlooking, charitably, the question of whether many women go to decorators to please their families, we pass on the word that this firm received more reader inquiries on a certain child's room reproduced in a *New York Times* home-furnishings spread than on anything it had had in the papers in years. The room cost, give or take a few small optionals, between $3,000 and $4,000. (The *Times'* editors also report, by the way, that they get more reader mail on children's rooms than on any other; kitchens come next.)

From B. Altman, the staid Fifth Avenue burgher, comes news that parents furnishing an infant's room today show an increasing tendency to decorate it impeccably in style with the rest of the house. "We have," says a buyer, "children's furniture in Colonial, French Provincial, Italian Provincial, various modern and other periods." He says that the average crib sold is between $60 and $75, but that the store has had a considerable success with such delicacies as a hand-painted four-poster job at $150, obviously a precursor of the canopy bed.

A small trend, among parents who can afford it, is the use of antiques in the children's quarters, and one Manhattan observer has noted that the Parke-Bernet Galleries are awash, of a frequent Saturday, with young matrons looking for antique cribs and rockers for their offspring. ("They like those antique touches to 'soften' the children's rooms," says a decorator, and adds, "The kids generally are allowed only to sleep in such rooms. They have someplace else to play.")

Since the youngster tucked into one of those frail beauties surely sleeps no better than he would in a paint-it-yourself model, it follows that such furnishings aren't being bought for Baby. But the ladies who buy them don't do the dusting themselves, and their numbers are limited. Far more common in home furnishings today is the subservience of adult tastes to children's requirements. This form of child worship hits almost every young parent who furnishes a home on a budget, and involves what may be designated The Child-Proof School of Homefurnishings.

Child-proof furniture is merchandise that has been plasticized, laminated, veneered, ironized, aluminized, asphalt-tile-ized, metal-frame-ized and otherwise sterilized beyond all aesthetic consideration. Typical is the chest of drawers "to grow with" (extra drawers magically appear as the child grows taller) that is set in a metal frame and covered with some plastic laminent, producing an effect smacking faintly of hospital wards and business offices.

There are the myriad wall and floor coverings that are scrubbable, scuffable, biteable, inkable, torturable, and generally practical to the point of consummate boredom. Such stuff, when it isn't called "child-proof," is "maintenance-free." "All this maintenance business happened mostly because of kids," says a builder. "These materials are permanent and very expensive. You can't change your color scheme once they're up. You're stuck with it. But people use them because of the children, and if they didn't have children I think the stuff would die. It's sure got nothing on pushing your heels into a nice thick wall-to-wall, let me tell you."

Parents, he says, are "maintenance-happy," which means that children today affect the furnishing of the home to an extraordinary degree. "If we're contemplating using a light-colored paper on the living-room walls," says a decorator, "our client will say, 'No, I love it but I can't have it with all my kids around. The walls would be filthy in no time.' What's happened, anyway? In the old days she would have used the paper and told the kids, 'Keep your grubby paws off it.' "

One housewife, sitting in the midst of her stolidly child-proofed domain, glumly surveys the plastic cups with which her two-year-old is playing, the cork floor on which her four-year-old is banging his head, the militantly modern, ruggedly brown sofa on which her seven-year-old has propped his feet, and speaks her mind:

"See this kitchen wallpaper? I hate it. I bought it because it's washable. There was another pattern I adored, but it wasn't washable. See these dishes? I detest plastic. All the dishes except my company set are plastic. We eat like peasants. Most of the furniture is plastic-surfaced, too. For years I dreamed of having an all-sea-green living room with an oyster-white sofa. It was a big thing with me. I'd lie awake nights and dream about a living room just the way I wanted it, with this oyster-white sofa sitting on a sea of sea-green broadloom. Hah!

"Oh, Lord, am I tired of practicality. But the only alternative was to make the living room off-limits to the kids, and we couldn't do that. Twenty years later they'd be telling their analysts how we rejected them."

Child-proof furnishings are almost always modern, and the editor of a home-decorating magazine has suggested that one big reason modern furniture may have had such overwhelming acceptance was not because all the adults who bought it necessarily liked it, but because children couldn't hurt it as they could period furniture. True, manufacturers have created the best of both worlds with such laboratory miracles as nylon velvet and plastic-coated satin, but these compromises somehow take the sport out of it. "Until the children are grown," says this editor, "parents cannot have their home as *they* might really like it."

One decorator, as resigned as her clientele, says flatly that her home offends her every professional sensibility. She has four children. "I feel like screaming whenever I look at a plastic surface, but what else can I do?" (One hears, faintly, echoes of that archaic refrain: "Keep your grubby paws off it!")

"When my youngest turns sixteen," she continues, in dizzied anticipation, "I'll lose my head. This whole damn place is going to be Louis XV and carpeted in pink, including the bathrooms, and there won't be a thing in it that isn't wildly perishable."

Meanwhile, the whole school of "maintenance-free" materials abounds and multiplies. Women's-page writers compose eulogies to them by day and go home at night to pound impotently on formica-topped tables. Distinctive and ornamental effects *can* be achieved with child-proofing, of course, but it takes talent. Too often, the maintenence-free home—furnished in modern, carpeted in tile, walled in something washable, upholstered in something rugged as an Army blanket, color-schemed to meet the challenge of tiny hands and feet, and offering up vast veneered expanses shorn of cozy baubles and gewgaws—meets the eye in a grimly predictable form. "Beauty," an interior designer says sourly, "has suffered in favor of what is durable and replaceable. All these things are inevitable in a child-centered society."

The final epitaph comes from Mr. Edward D. Stone, builder of embassies, proponent of graciousness, mourner for the lost age of elegance, and a man whose horror of the maintenance-free school of living shines through his surface control as clearly as the rays of sunlight through one of his filigree walls.

"Parents today," says Mr. Stone, "do a home that can be hosed down like a latrine. They have sacrificed all elegance to their children.

"This craze for informality, wherein kids and dogs have *carte blanche* privilege in the home, is an excuse for laziness. It is obviously easier to feed kids hamburgers in the back yard than to sit at a dining room table and hold a coherent conversation. It is obviously easier to do away with things that are valuable and attractive than to teach children to respect them.

"Much of this informal business stems from"—the word passes his lips reluctantly—"California. Look at some of those awful development homes. They have discarded Colonial architecture, which had grace and formality. The plan—a central hall, a living room, a formal dining room, a kitchen at the rear—it imposed certain niceties and disciplines on the family. What have we today? Ranch houses finished with hair-shirt materials, floors covered in"—venomously—"asphalt tile, the kitchen opening into the family room, the family room into the living room—all living together, in a glorified hovel, with no reprieve from the children. The kids yell, the TV blares, the dogs bark."

Breathing deeply, he moves on to the final assault: "We are the richest people in the world. We are supposed to be world leaders. Our object should be to produce cultivated, well-mannered adults. Instead we are turning loose a race of barbarians. We are the sloppiest people in the world, and it all comes from our graceless, careless, so-called informal home life."

Mr. Stone is cheered by the intelligence that the separate dining room has been making a small comeback in recent seasons. But he brightens only fleetingly, sensing perhaps that no mere dining room will stem the inexorable tide of asphalt tile. He taps a fingernail (buffed) upon a table top (teak), sounding out the toll of the bells. "Long Island," he says darkly, "Long Island is doomed."

IN SCHOOL

The Cold War

The question is: If the good forebears of the P.T.A.—
first gathered, on Feb. 17, 1897, in solemn conclave in Washington, D.C., to set forth the aims and goals of what was
then known as the National Congress of Mothers—if they
were around today (and some may be) to note the fruits of
their heroic labors, could they stand their own success?

The P.T.A. now has more than twelve million card-carry-
ing members, of whom three and a half million are men—a
statistic over which its founders would rejoice—and some
800,000 teachers and school administrators, which inspires
a certain ambivalence on both sides of the fence. There are
some 47,000 Parent-Teacher Associations distributed through
every state and just about every American military base extant. In short, wherever the nation's flag flies, the P.T.A. is
not far behind.

It had, of course, a right good start. Those Gay Nineties which saw the birth of the P.T.A. also spawned the formalized beginnings of progressive education. They were made for each other, dedicated as both were to the premise that the best way to bring forth a child with a Sound Mind in a Sound Body was for parent and teacher, home and school, to join hands and hold on tight.

If, ever since, teachers have sometimes wished they could let go, parents have only tightened their grip until in many communities today they have achieved a half nelson. "I suppose the parents here would have enough power to get me fired if they really wanted to," cautiously concedes an elementary school principal in one rich, smallish, heavily child-oriented suburb, "but I would *hope* our relationship is amicable enough so we could sit down and talk things over before they tried."

A far cry, this, from the days when a principal was lord of his manor. Today the notion that a parent gets into the act only when his child is in trouble is as quaint as the one-room school. The classrooms are aswarm with room mothers; the teachers are summoned to dinner at their pupils' homes. ("Twenty years ago," one says, "the parent wouldn't have had the nerve to invite me. Today they invite me and I haven't got the nerve to say no.") The guidance counselor is booked to capacity with parent conferences; Board of Education meetings play to standing room only; the principal, if he hasn't completely capitulated to the parent body, at least remembers to say "please" when he asks folks to keep their hands off the curriculum. Most of the old relationships between home and school have been turned upside down and inside out, and probably never will be the same again.

When one mentions "schooling," one hits a prime parental nerve. The child-centered parent may state his position clearly

—implicitly—in the home and in the community, but it is in the school that the wraps really come off. There all the manifest aggression *verboten* in polite adult society is not only acceptable, but desirable. There the parent—otherwise aware of, even amused by, her own child-centeredness—metamorphoses into a lioness defending her cub. To question her presence in that particular den is unwise. Admiral Hyman Rickover, frequent commentator on the state of American education and a brave man, learned this some months ago when he said publicly of the P.T.A.'ers, "They're an infernal nuisance. They ought to stay home and take care of their husbands." The admiral's restraint in the face of the furor that followed was surely the better part of valor.

Now, obviously it is far better for parents to overinvolve themselves in school matters than not to involve themselves at all. Nobody—not even the teacher who bemoans the eagle-eyed mamas peering over her shoulder—would call this bad. But one may wonder, nonetheless, just what is going on that makes so very many people so very hot under the collar when it comes to the education of their offspring.

"It's a cold war," says a school psychiatrist who has warmed the inhospitable wooden seats of many a P.T.A. conclave. "The parents feel the only way they can function is by being strong enough to stand up to the teachers and say, 'No, we don't agree with you.' The teachers feel the only way they can function is by being strong enough to stand up to the parents and say the same thing. Mostly, these mothers are so wrapped up in their children that everything else is secondary. They have made their kids little kings in the house, and they want them to be little kings in the school. They come prepared to fight. Sometimes they don't really have anything to fight for, just a vague notion that their kids have a divine right to the best of everything and, by damn, if they are *good* mothers

—and many of them aren't at all sure they are—they should fight to get it. The P.T.A. is full of rebels without a cause."

"Only the best" is an oft-heard phrase in the P.T.A. William Whyte cites an illuminating example in his book, *The Organization Man*. Discussing the worldly aspirations of the surburbanites of Park Forest, Illinois, he says: ". . . Park Foresters demanded that a special $60,000 multi-purpose room be added to a new school then abuilding. [Town autorities] said no; eventually the town was going to have to take over the financial burden and it was questionable whether they would have the tax base to pay for the regular classrooms, let alone the extra facilities. I asked the young head of the school board about this. With great heat, he declared that it was a matter of principle. 'Our children deserve the best,' he said, and since a multi-purpose room was part of modern education, that should be that. I asked him about [the authorities'] argument. He shook his head sadly; he didn't know where the money would come from either. 'But,' he repeated, 'our children deserve the best.' To ask why, of course, would be unpardonable in suburbia."

Unpardonable—but not just in surburbia. When it comes to schooling, parental loss of humor is pandemic—and sometimes very humorous indeed. As witness:

The meeting of a Board of Education in an upper-middle-class New England community, one evening not too long ago, in a school auditorium. Parents fill the room and overflow into SRO, for it is a very special meeting. The issue at hand: An elementary school is overcrowded. Funds for a new school cannot be voted until election time, a year hence, since a public referendum is required for any structure over $100,000. That means the school is at least two years away from completion. Meanwhile, what to do? A committee of the board is about to make its recommendation.

The chairman, seated with his colleagues on the stage, looks the crowd over uneasily. The natives, he sees, are restless tonight. He clears his throat, and speaks:

"Now, I know you folks feel strongly about this thing, and I want to assure you that after the committee makes its report you'll all get a chance to be heard. I just want to ask, *please,* folks, that you restrict yourselves to legitimate questions and constructive suggestions. Otherwise we'll be here all night. Remember last year?" He smiles unhappily. "Now, then."

The committee recommendation is made. The plan, obviously based on exhaustive research and illustrated by a big, gorgeous map showing school zones and population distribution, is to transfer 109 children from the overcrowded school into two other schools, transporting them by bus. It is greeted by screaming silence. Finally a woman raises her hand and is recognized.

"I'd like to know how long," she says, hands on hips in warning, "*exactly how long* those bus rides are going to be." About fifteen minutes, the board's traffic expert tells her. There is a loud gasp of disbelief from the audience. Well, he says, fingering his tie, it was clocked during moderate traffic hours; perhaps twenty minutes in heavy traffic.

"It is a half-hour ride," the lady says accusingly. "*At least* half an hour. A six-year-old child cannot sit on a swaying bus for forty-five minutes twice a day and stay alert. They will be exhausted in class. Have you thought of *that?*"

The audience murmurs approvingly. The board agrees to reclock the travel time. Another hand is raised: "How about the psychological effect of the move on our children? How about the trauma?"

Why should there be trauma? she is asked. "Well, because," she says. "Because. The books say elementary school children should not be shifted around. It makes them insecure. How do you *know* there would be no trauma?"

The audience growls. The chairman nods quickly to a woman up front. She rises and turns to face the crowd.

"My children have had to change schools four times," she says, "and I don't believe it produced any traumas. I think"— she smiles apologetically—"that it depends on the attitude of the parents. If the parents relax, the move needn't be so bad for the children. We can even make it fun for them, treating it as a new adventure." She is loudly booed down and slinks, purple-faced, into her seat.

Another woman jumps up. She is shaking with wrath. "My Lord," she says, "how Pollyanna can you get? It may be fine for *your* wonderful children, but for you to say that *any* child can be moved four times without trauma is *sheer nonsense. My* child was seriously affected in his relationship with his sibling. It is just getting back to normal, and *I don't want him traumatized again.*" She sits down, still shaking, to a large, sympathtic ovation.

The P.T.A. president (a man; this is not uncommon in heavily child-fixated communities), who has until now been conferring quietly with aides to his left and right, rather like a U.N. delegate before his major speech, solemnly stands up. "It seems to me you fellows are looking for easy solutions," he says. "We are not interested in easy solutions. We are interested in *children.* [Applause.] Now, if all you want to do is solve this thing easily let's just take 109 children and shoot them. [Laughter.] . . . You are not going to railroad us. This plan is not acceptable. We will form a committee . . ." Applause and several choruses of "Hear, hear" drown out the rest of his sentence.

The chairman gavels for order. "Please, folks!" he says.

"Please! Remember that we asked for constructive suggestions. Does anyone have a constructive suggestion?"

An eminently reasonable-looking chap raises his hand and is hastily recognized. "Mr. Chairman," he says,"I am President of the Sunny Side Homes Association. We have prepared a short statement which I would like to read at this time."

The chairman nods approval. The speaker launches into an interminable account of the educational tribulations that children of the Sunny Side Homes have had to endure over the years. ". . . And now," he winds up, "we face these dreadful extensive round trips, maybe to the other end of town, for our small ones. In all fairness, must our youngsters be called upon to face additional sacrifice?"

Applause. The chairman rises with a look of infinite determination. "Folks," he says, "I tell you truly, I think we have studied every possible alternative. If you will just look at this map—"

From the back of the hall comes a shout: *"My children are not pinheads on a map!"* Cheers break out. This one has struck home; the crowd tastes blood. The chairman bangs his gavel frantically. "Please, people!" he yells. "Please, people!" But he has clearly lost control. He shrugs helplessly and adjourns the meeting until next week.

The following week, after four hours of testy bickering and several near-disastrous clashes between mothers, the original committee recommendation is passed. With echoes of fury still lingering in the air, a parent dressed in a Boy Scout troop leader's uniform rises. "Mr. Chairman," he says, "we know you all worked mighty hard on this thing, and that you did the best you could for our children. And I think I am speaking for all the parents here when I say we want to thank you for a job well done." A barely respectable round

of applause indicates that the spokesman is self-appointed. The
chairman, however, is visibly touched. "Thank you," he says.
"There have been people here who have spoken in temper or
anguish. And this is perfectly understandable. After all, our
children are involved . . ."

Later, he said privately: "As far as we can tell, the primary
reason for all the anger is inconvenience to the parents. From
our observations, the elementary children adjust very quickly
to switching schools, and they certainly don't mind getting
on a bus. But the *parents* mind. It means they have to drive
several miles after school to pick their children up for dancing
classes or music lessons. It means the children make friends
who live further away, and when they visit each other the
parents have to drive them back and forth—that sort of thing.

"Then, too, we find that parents come prepared to be
belligerent, no matter what the issue is. Their attitude is,
'Nobody's going to push *my* child around,' even when nobody
has any such intention. You know, we have one of the best
public school systems in New England. [True]. Many, many
parents move here at great financial sacrifice [the average purchase price of houses in the community is $25,000] just for
the schools. We have about 12,000 children in twenty-one
schools. We employ 766 people in the school system. Around
580 of them are teachers and guidance counselors. The average class size is twenty-five, and very few classes go over
thirty. There are no double sessions. We have all this, and
yet if you listen to the parents, everything we do is bad. If a
class goes up to twenty-eight instead of twenty-six, they
gripe about inferior instruction. If we bus some children
from one excellent school to another excellent school to bring
the level back to twenty-six, they gripe about the bus ride. If
we tried to discontinue the bus service—boy, would they yell!
Parents are always griping, just on general principles."

When it comes to the schools, every issue is a burning issue. In some quarters this makes enthusiasm hard to sustain. "At first," says a past president, now flagrantly inactive, of one P.T.A. unit, "you're full of spirit because you feel strongly about education and you want to help insure that your children get the best. The first year we had our new school, the parents were fired with enthusiasm—everything for our children. But after a while we felt like a group without any reason for being. Once I asked another mother, 'What is our *purpose?*' and she said, 'Damned if I know.' That was the trouble. We had none. I mean, sure, there *are* noble purposes—the National Congress states them, and they appear in all our literature, and they sound great—but they are so nebulous. It was great to say we were helping educate our children, but when it came right down to it our purpose seemed to be raising money to fix a creaking door here, replace a sofa in a teachers' lounge there. It wasn't especially ennobling.

"Sometimes I felt the teachers hated the P.T.A. They hated the parents keeping an eye on them. I think they would consider it ideal if they could have no contact with it, except to use the money it raises."

Much P.T.A. time and effort is in fact devoted to fund-raising. Card nights are one common method. Children's fashion shows are extremely popular, though there is always the danger, as in one recent fiasco, that the parents of those not modeling may stay away. The money may be used for the P.T.A. Council, a scholarship fund, student organizations; and often to purchase those little extras that, as Boards of Education generally fail to realize, make life worthwhile—such as television sets or band uniforms for the school. But there comes a point at which even parents balk. In one community, for example, a new principal requested a silver tea service which could be used in the teachers' lounge and at P.T.A. meetings. A few mothers were for it, holding that the private school esprit thus established somehow would transmit itself to the children; but the majority turned the request down cold. ("We might have considered silverplate," one mother said, "but sterling!")

Despite such frippery, not even the most severely disenchanted could deny the enormous body of good, solid work accomplished by local P.T.A.'s. P.T.A. citizens' committees have researched school curricula and sat down with teachers to work out revised, generally superior, courses of study. Many have lobbied successfully for more comprehensible marking systems. They support school bond issues, they are involved in federal aid to education, and they struggle with such serious concerns as the "drop-out" problem by trying to find part-time or summer employment for underprivileged youngsters. They work tirelessly as volunteers, usually in school libraries, for which they also raise funds, and their record on raising safety standards is, of course, peerless. And if the non-P.T.A. world chooses to smile indulgently at them, it is only because of the Helen Hokinsonian milieu they have somehow created, and because of that relentless humorlessness that pervades so many of their causes and caucuses.

For example, the safety issue. In one town the parents formed a committee to campaign for a second roadway in front of the elementary school. They claimed that the traffic-jammed street, with small children scooting between the automobiles, constituted a safety hazard, and clamored for a Police Department investigation. They got it and it revealed:

(1) that the traffic jam was due entirely to parents' cars dropping off the children and picking them up;

(2) that the hazard was vastly increased on rainy days, when mothers would leave their cars double- and triple-parked while they ran into the school building with boots, slickers,

and umbrellas, to escort their gossamer young back to the cars;

(3) that almost all the children thus chauffeured were exempt from bus service because they lived within easy walking distance (one-half-mile radius) of the school.

Thus the traffic hazard. Did the parents find any irony in the situation? Not at all. They went right ahead, won their case, and now, on rainy days, *two* roadways are clogged with parent traffic.

Even the essentially morbid may be crossed with inadvertent humor when P.T.A. sights are trained on it. Last winter, during a short national flurry of revived interest in fallout shelters, the agenda at one parent-teacher board meeting proceeded like this: an upcoming father-daughter party ("Shall we use snowball cut-outs or lollipop cut-outs for place cards?"); distribution of accolades with regard to a recent school play ("I move we have it written into the minutes to thank the mothers for the beautiful job they did on pressing all those red bows for the children"); school maintenance ("The second floor is being painted, but I see straws in the wind that the men will be pulled off the job before it is done; *we must make sure they complete the work!*"); and, finally, fallout shelters.

The question was whether to press for a school shelter or unite with all the other P.T.A.'s in town to take up cudgels for community shelters.

A member nixed the school shelter because, she pointed out, adults coming to pick up the children might crowd the kiddies out.

Another nixed community shelters because, by the time the children got to them, they might be filled to capacity with adults.

A woman said, "Anyway, do we need a school shelter? I

read that in case of nuclear attack, all children will be dismissed."

Another said, "And supposing we're bombed on a Saturday or Sunday? What good is a school shelter then?"

The principal then volunteered to invite a local expert in these matters, a retired colonel, to render his opinion at the next available P.T.A. meeting. But when?

"Let's see, now," said the president. "We have our February dance, and then we don't have anything scheduled in March or April. But March is no good because that's Lent, and we never get a good turnout during Lent. How about"—she looked up brightly—"how about May? We need someone for the May meeting anyway."

May, then, for the colonel. Everyone agreed he would draw an excellent crowd ("After all, we're interested not so much for ourselves, but for our *children*"), and the meeting was promptly adjourned.

P.T.A.'ers thus convened in pursuit of the best for their young have a boundless capacity for playing it straight:

In an Ohio town a group spends two hours analyzing an article from an educational journal, a most scholarly treatise of several thousand words devoted to the efficacy of hand-raising in class (the parents conclude, with its author, that this is an "undemocratic" teaching process; the teachers present play it close to the vest). In Connecticut a teacher is fired, courtesy of the P.T.A., for clipping, on the backside and not too hard, a child who wouldn't stop clipping *her*. In Massachusetts a gathering of P.T.A. mothers sits enchanted through a lecture entitled, "Are Fathers Necessary?" And, again in Massachusetts, they have a rousing battle over the teaching methods of a new mathematics man. One mother reports his system is "traumatizing my child." Another says,

"He seems like an awfully good father image to me, that's all I can say."

In a Connecticut city, entirely at the behest of parents, teachers are instructed by the superintendent of schools not to discuss nuclear war in class; if students ask questions, he says, the teacher should agree it is an important matter and say he hopes the class can talk about it later in the year. In New York a woman has to resign her presidency of a P.T.A. chapter because her husband objects; she seldom gets to see him or the children. ("Often," says an educator, "the child comes home to get his own food out of the refrigerator while mom is out saving the school system.") From Brooklyn, word comes of a courageous loner who quit the P.T.A. because "the girls refused to broaden their horizons. . . . I told them we couldn't help ourselves unless we help others," she said. "I told them, 'We say we need a new school. Ten blocks away they need a new school, too. Now why don't we think about this and examine our needs and theirs and see where it is really needed more.' And they jumped on me and yelled, 'What do you mean, needed more? *Our children come first.*' They were so hostile, I felt completely rejected and went and told the principal I had decided to quit." (Faintly, faintly come to mind noble words from *Where Children Come First*, a purple eulogy to the P.T.A. founders authored by Harry and Bonaro Overstreet: ". . . Here the basic principle was expressed: not 'myself first' or 'our own children first' but 'ourselves all together' . . .").

In Glencoe, Illinois, parents are invited to design report cards if none of the available types meets with their liking. "It gives me a secure feeling," a mother says, "to know that my child's teacher wants me to know the truth, and that I can decide how I should receive it."

Parents will go to extraordinary lengths to make sure no little ids are injured in the classroom. In one school the teaching staff, sated with "parental nagging," as one teacher called it, decided to give the folks plenty of rope. It invited them over for a "Parents Go to School" night wherein they would play pupil. Greeting them in the gym before they marched off to their assignments, the principal said: "I'll say to you as I do to the children: You look ready to learn. You're big enough. And you *look* smart enough!"

In the modern math class, a teacher guided twenty parents through the mysteries of quadratic equations. Departing from his role for a moment, he told them, "Most of my pupils have discovered the secret of these equations. Just one hasn't." No sooner had the bell rung than every parent was at his elbow, wanting to know if hers was the hapless child. His smile was serene and supremely noncommital.

In the art class, the parents dabbed self-consciously in finger paints. To one, the teacher said, "Ah, I see you are an admirer of Mondrian—just like Peter," and the parent dissolved into a plasm of pleasure. Every other parent, the teacher could surely see, awaited similar comment. She profferred none.

In the physical education class, a spry young specimen in tights had nine parents, including two portly gentlemen with jackets doffed, doing some brisk calisthenics. The group obviously was expiring fast, but the young teacher was relentless. *"Drop* your head, 1, 2, 3, 4," she said. *"Touch* your toe, 1, 2, 3, 4." One of the men stumbled toward a chair. "Oh, *come* now," she said, infinitely guileless, "you don't want me to tell your little boy you couldn't keep up with him, do you?" And she launched them into a folk dance step. "Now," she said, "I think you are all so talented we will put it to music."

And, "*Left* foot, *right* foot, sing, SING! A big black dog sat on the back porch and Bingo was his name . . ."

A principal elsewhere, told of the Parents Go to School evening, laughed happily. "You don't often get opportunities like that," she said. "We no longer have a situation where we can invite the parents into the school and stand up and tell them. They tell us. It is a delicate situation. Parents have every nerve exposed about their children's schooling, and we have to be immensely tactful. If anything goes wrong in school, they never blame the child—they blame the school.

"They feel so guilty. They worry about whether they're doing the right thing with their children and they suspect they're not. Fully as much of our time is spent with parents as with the children. They call me at home incessantly. They talk about the school and their children and the school and their children. I suppose we'd rather have them like this than totally disinterested, but—face it: they can be a pain in the neck.

"We once had a visitor from the London school system who told me, 'In England, parents and dogs are not allowed in the schools.' Horrible attitude, isn't it? But sometimes, when the tenth mother has come into this office and used up a box of Kleenex telling me she's not child-centered, I wish—at least I *think* I wish—I worked there."

"I hate to see the parents socially," says a teacher. "They back me up against a wall and I can't escape. Are the kids getting enough science. Are they getting too much homework. What's wrong with the P.T.A. What's wrong with the Board of Education. Are we too permissive. Are we too tough. Are we putting enough stress on individual achievement. Are we putting enough stress on group achievement. Should they switch to private school. How are all their little psyches doing. Well, I tell you, I'm in the school dealing with those little psyches all day long, and in the evening I'd damn well like to switch to something else. If I didn't think education was important I wouldn't be a teacher. But too much is too much. These parents, they're all school-crazy, that's what."

With parents thus afflicted, teachers nowadays have less cause to complain of absenteeism. Where pupils live too close to school to get bussed, the car pools go forth under climatic conditions that would stagger a postman. "There was one morning last winter we found several tons of snow in the driveway," a suburban husband recalls somberly. "I decided not even to try to get into the office before noon. I wouldn't have gone to the doorstep for a newspaper, but my wife tells me to start shoveling, she's got to get the kid to school. I said, 'What's the big deal? The kid's in first grade. Why can't she miss a day?' My wife is horrified. 'Are you crazy?' she says. 'It's *school*, that's why.' 'So what?' I say. 'What will happen— she'll flunk *sandpile* or something?' And you know what she said? She said, 'Listen, Dave, you've got a very negative attitude. If you want this child to get to college you better start shoveling.' "

No, absenteeism is not the sort of thing that the child worshiper is lenient about. She does, however, want to know that the school sees things her way—i.e., that it takes full cognizance of all her child's "rights." And, generally, it does.

In the heady climate of democracy, nobody is surprised any more when high-schoolers draft and vote on their own disciplinary codes: on whether or not they should smoke in school or hold hands in class, and on how informally they may dress. But an interviewer is brought up short to find that in one elementary school even the third-graders have formulated and put to class vote their own rules of behavior. The teacher says: "I find it's easier on their nerves and on mine."

A fifth-grade teacher carries the democratic process somewhat further: his class is run not only democratically, but by the proudest tenets of capitalism. Pupils are graded in terms of money: $10,000 for an "A" paper, $8,000 for "B," and so on, down to insolvency. The class has a "bank," a Sears Roebuck catalogue, a shopping center, mock money, and mock checks. The money, tax deducted first, is duly deposited, and the children then draw freely on their accounts, making their selections from the catalogue and placing their orders (any item over $100 is paid for by check) in the shopping center.

"You should hear them when they make a killing on a test," the teacher says. "They rush right to the catalogue yelling, 'Today I'm going to buy Mommy a mink coat!' Of course, we have to deal in large amounts to keep the operation going." There is a commotion in the bank, and he calls across the room: "Aw, please, you guys, can't you settle down?"— then turns back to the economic truths at hand.

"The other teachers sometimes criticize this system," he says. "They ask, 'How much respect will these kids have for a $5 bill when they grow older?' And I suppose they have a point. But *my* point is, *are these kids motivated!* They knock themselves out studying to get the extra $1,000 on an assignment. They are having *fun* while learning. That's *my* point."

And a number of parents with youngsters in the class feel it's quite a good one. "I don't care about anything else," one mother says, "so long as my child is happy."

"The parents do a great deal of talking about education," says a guidance counselor, "but I think many of them are more concerned about adjustment."

"From the beginning," says William Whyte, turning again to his Park Foresters, "the curriculum has borne down very heavily on the pragmatic and the social, and the concept of adjustment has been dominant . . . For what is it that parents

want most emphasized by the school? . . . When they wrote
the answer in their own words, one note was found more often
than any other. The primary job of the high school, they
wrote, should be to teach students how to be citizens and how
to get along with other people."

An educator tells of a woman who approached him, after
he had addressed a parents' meeting, in a state of great agi-
tation. The local school principal, she told him, had advised
her to withdraw her daughter from class for a time; the girl
was "not showing sufficient group spirit" and was "acting
immature."

How old was the child?

"Five," said the woman.

At a New York private school, a four-year-old was turned
down although he had a high I.Q. and his brother was an
alumnus. Reason: the boy wasn't "aggressive enough." "We're
attuned to a more outgoing personality here," a teacher told
the crushed parents. "The whole tenor of the group is outgoing. Your child wouldn't be happy here. He just wouldn't
fit."

"The trouble is, every mother who once had a psych course
and every teacher thinks she's an analyst," says a school psychologist. Indeed, the analytic current is powerful. P.T.A.
meetings provide abundant yields of quasi-psychiatric jargon,
in which "aggressive," "withdrawn," "adjustment," and
"group" figure strongly and "peers" is a very big word indeed.
Individual parent-teacher conferences list heavily in this direction, as, of course, does the whole cult of "testing."

But despite the marked psychiatric flavor, P.T.A. times have
changed drastically since a mere decade ago, when the child's
psyche was the first order of business. Today's child worshiper
wants her offspring happy, healthy, democratized, and adjusted, but she also wants him to go to college. The public

schools do their best to cope with this dual parental drive; but to find the people who are ministering to the child's needs, academic and psychiatric, more zealously than anyone else around, one must turn to the private schools. Here is something bigger than the P.T.A.—bigger, even, than parents, who, knowing college competition for the cutthroat affair it is, express their anxiety early. "I am concerned with how he does in kindergarten now," one mother says, "because of college." And nothing gives a child a better headstart in this bruising competition than a private school diploma.

There are around 1,000 private schools affiliated with the National Association of Independent Schools and a goodly number unaffiliated, and, to no one's surprise, almost every one of them is filled to absolute capacity.

Traditionally, the private school body is composed of children and siblings of alumni, children of those with friends in high places, such as the Board of Trustees, and, now and again, children of those with no ties more potent than money, social or professional status, or a powerful lot of luck. A few scholarship youngsters generally have rounded out the enrollment, thus bathing the select proceedings in a warm republican light.

Time marches. There has been no dramatic upsurge in the number of private school students in the country—there is no room for them—but the upsurge in applications from a vast corps of middle-class citizenry that suddenly has come to consider private schooling one of the necessities of life is fantastic. One exclusive boys' school that admits ninety first-graders each year had, a decade ago, 85 applications; last year, two months before the deadline for applications, it had 590 and the mail was growing heavier daily. A girls' school received more than 600 applications for 70 available places. Another, 350 applications, of which only 30 could be accepted.

Many parents claim they would not seek private schooling for their young if the public schools met the same high standards, and some of them mean it. But even in the densely populated cities, where private schooling may be considered very nearly essential, they may have other motives. And when they live in areas where the public school systems are top-rated, the motives are plain. First, of course, status appeal: Here is one of the few remaining status symbols that still eludes the grasp of the merely loaded, and the mother who can say, "My son is coming home from New Haven for the holidays," is way ahead of the game. Or, as Fred Hechinger, the education editor of *The New York Times*, has pointed out, "If everyone goes to college, you've got to make up for that equalization by sending your child to a *better* college. Thus, the Ivy League rat race." (Ivy League hysteria, he says, is peculiar to the Eastern provinces. An exception is Texas, which loves to send its daughters to a snazzy Eastern school for two years of finishing, and then bring them home to Texas universities where they may be safely married off to solvent he-men, a type not so readily found, apparently, up North.)

Then there is the private school's high batting average in the Ivy League. It is estimated that students in the top 5 per cent of a public high school stand a good chance of breaking the Ivy League barrier; in a good private school those chances are better than sporting for the *upper half* of the graduating class.

So beseiged are the privates that it is today not a luxury but a privilege to be accepted by one of them, and a privilege for which astonishing numbers of parents are willing to pay far, far beyond their means. Tuitions climb from about $250 a year for day students in the private neighborhood schools in most big cities, to $2,000 and $3,000 for live-ins in the truly plush academies, which are concentrated heavily in New York and New England. It is at these top schools, of course, that the demand is greatest and gate-crashing hardest. Many of them are so inundated with gentry that few parents, except those who themselves labored in these serene ivied halls, even bother to apply. But for the good, expensive, high-status private school which still maintains at least an aura of availability, middle-class competition is as fierce as for any college.

Most have their particular appeals and, through the years, have evolved personalities which the school-wise mother knows as well as the personalities of her own family. At one, the teaching is "tense." At another, it is "relaxed." Word moves fast around the cocktail-party and charity-lunch circuit about the relative debits and credits of each school, about what teacher inhibits the children and what teacher makes them feel at ease with their peers and what headmaster is having difficulty with what instructor who is not so strong on remedial reading. When a new school opens, all eyes turn to it. The mothers have the lowdown immediately, and considered guesses are passed around about whether to forget it or to join the applicants in the long, long line that forms to the right. "These bits of luncheon gossip can make or break a new school," says a headmaster. "And they keep the rest of us on our toes. We try to avoid any radical move. Once a school is typed it's very hard to change the image."

In New York—a small town in such matters—the images are ironclad. Dalton is known among initiates as progressive and democratic. The Town School is called "progressive in learning and conservative in behavior"—a marvelously safe role for any school to play. Brearley has scholarship, conservatism; children in the lower classes have been known to curtsey when bidding their teachers good-bye. Spence and Chapin are considered more proper yet, though one wonders how much further propriety can go. ("They raise *good* girls," a close observer explains, "whereas Brearley also raises *girls*.")

Brearley also is known, justifiably or not, as a school whose girls "grow up to be Radcliffe girls—aggressive, positive types." Thus it made perfect sense to her social circle when a woman with four daughters enrolled at Brearley reconsidered and took them out, one by one. An acquaintance with two girls of her own in the school, shaken by the mass retreat, asked why the four had been removed. "Nancy," said the lady, "I don't have an answer, I have a question: Whom do Brearley girls marry?" "I don't know," said Nancy. "Whom do they marry?" "That's just the point," the woman answered. "You don't know. *That's* why I took them out!"

While each of the private schools may have its distinct characteristics, they divide, in another sense, into two broad categories: the professionally exclusive and the professionally democratic, and it is not easy to say which is snippier. The first, a relatively small group, caters to the noblest names in Dun & Bradstreet and in the prestige professions, making no bones about it and handing out, to preserve a united social front, a few scholarships to the offspring of impoverished gentry. Their emphasis is on tradition, decorum, and academic achievement. They are disinclined to ponder their own snobberies forthrightly, tending instead to view themselves as the last frontier in a fine but largely unfashionable cause. "The only purpose of a private school," says one spokesman, "is that it deals in excellence—of all sorts." "The virtue of good private school teachers is that when they speak of *Alice in Wonderland*, they've *read* it," says another.

The professionally democratic schools, on the other hand, go out of their way to obtain "better ethnic distribution," and will often enroll under capacity to leave room for scholarship children of Negro or Oriental families. Wiseacres are wont to refer to this practice as the "token Negro policy," an accusation deeply resented by the schools. "We do seek a balance," says a headmistress, only a trifle defensively, "and when we can't get that balance through applications, we go out and look for the children to achieve it."

Often 25 per cent, and sometimes more, of the children in these schools, have some form of reduced tuition. The general atmosphere is more permissive, the curricula are more progressive, and academic achievement, while valued, gives up some ground to social adjustment. At one such school a mother found out just how much may have to be given up. "Tommy was in the nursery grade," she says. "He was four. He had this teacher, a young girl who had come in from the public school system, who told me that he had amazing powers of concentration; he would sit and stick to one project for two hours at a time. He desperately wanted to learn to read, and this girl tried to help him. But the school wouldn't let her. They said it was too early. They said at this stage he should be developing his large muscles and learning to be social. The headmistress told her, 'No, you cannot teach him to read.' So she stopped, and by the time Tommy got to first grade he had lost his interest in reading. The teacher left eventually. She told me she couldn't stand it."

Tommy, however, stayed on, and crisis struck again. "When he was five," says his mother, "he started building lovely things and bringing them home. He'd cut out animals with a jigsaw, and make little boats with prows and decks and smokestacks. We were delighted. We figured we had this budding genius, and our older boy couldn't use his hands at all. Then Tommy got to be six, and suddenly his techniques started deteriorating. He began bringing home more and more things, bigger and bigger things, and they were no damn good. He'd stagger into the house with two great big pieces of wood nailed together and I'd say what is it and he'd say it's a boat. He'd come in with two even bigger pieces and I'd say what is this one and he'd say it's a plane. I'd say what kind of plane and he'd say oh, just a plane. The stuff kept getting bigger and bigger and worse and worse. Well, I thought about it a long time. I didn't want to discourage his creative streak, if there was any left, and I wanted to be accepted—*you* know. But finally I decided I had to express my judgment, even if I ran the risk of alienating him and ruining his genius for life. So I said, Listen, Tommy, this stuff really isn't worthy of you. You can do better. Why do you keep making it? What's it all about? And he said, Mommy, you just don't understand. I want to build a doghouse and *they won't let me.*"

While the exclusive school takes its nepotism with placidity, and even with satisfaction, the democratic school worries about it. "Of course, we can't say no to children or siblings of former pupils," says a member of the latter cult, "and we could easily fill up with psychiatrists' children—we seem to have a certain attraction for them." The fact puzzles her, but not unpleasantly. "It is not easy to keep a healthy balance."

Out of this competitive morass has come the Interview, a procedure designed to screen applicants, determine the desirability of parents and the "social maturity" of children, and to furnish the schools with a graceful way of studying the situation in depth before they say no. It can be, and for many parents is, a totally unnerving experience. Many testify to sleepless nights before an Interview, to putting their children through weeks of involved preparatory paces, to mounting panic as they wait for the school's decision. Mothers get their heads together in anxiety-ridden consultation over how to dress their tots for an Interview ("Keep him in an Eton suit, they like children looking spiffy"), how to dress themselves, whether or not to take their husbands along (highly recommended, the grapevine has it, at one school where the interviewer seems to relate better to men), what to say and how to say it. "You *know* it's ridiculous," says one mother who dragged her youngster around through five schools and seven hideous weeks before finally making the grade. "But you can't help getting anxious. Even the parents who recognize what nonsense all this is get caught up in it."

At the Interview itself a small child understandably may be thrown. Parent and child are greeted by the interviewer in an office containing, generally, a wide variety of playthings. It becomes crucially important that the child choose to occupy himself with the *right* plaything, i.e., a constructive one. The interviewer makes apparent small talk with the parent, and occasionally tosses a smile at the child, whom the parent is eying furtively ("Every time she looked toward him I thought, Oh God, David, don't be picking your nose"). The questions she asks of the little one sound aimless enough, but mama knows better. Eventually—this is the pattern in many schools —another teacher comes in. At least, she looks like another teacher. She is, in fact, the staff psychiatrist, or guidance director, whose purpose it is to trot the child off for further observation while the interviewer continues to work on mama. "How do you do, David," she says, and holds out her hand. "Won't you come with me and find some other toys?"

Now, there stands David, attacking a set of blocks or, heaven help him, cuddling a doll. He is in a strange building, his mother is obviously distraught, one strange lady is asking him funny questions and another is threatening to take him away from mama. Maybe he feels nervous. But the school holds that if David is a *socially mature* child he will get through. When an adult holds out a hand to a three-year-old and says good morning, and the tot holds out his hand with a smile and offers a sturdy shake—*that*, they say, is social maturity.

At some schools, the Interview is followed by an application for admission made out by the parents. Other schools, playing it cozier, work in reverse: no Interview until the application has been received and sized up. Some even require letters of recommendation—for the parents. Indeed, so much hangs upon the desirability of the parents that one mother has charged: "It's more a case of choosing the parents than choosing the children."

The unqualified independence of the schools lends a certain crustiness to the proceedings. "It would be revolutionary for a teacher to say, 'I hope you're interested in our school,' " says a parent. "Instead they say, 'I hope you've applied to lots of other schools.' "

A father recalls taking his daughter for an Interview when she was three. "The teacher and I sparred with great courtesy," he says. "And meanwhile we both eyed—she calmly, I nervously—what Claudia was doing with crayons. Then I got a look at the drawing Claudia had made. It was a face with no nose. I was horrified—what psychiatric deviation would the teacher read into this? I said—trying to keep it light, you know, as if I thought it was merely funny—I said, 'Oh, Claudia, where's the *nose?*' The teacher said, 'Now, now, now!' and she wagged her finger in my face playfully. 'You're *cheat*-ing!' Soon this other old dame came in and we were introduced and she said, 'Well, Claudia, how would you like to come and play?' And Claudia, who was an old hand at this game—it was her fourth interview—threw me a reassuring look and went off.

"Then the sparring really began. She asked about my

educational background; I asked how the school taught children to read. She asked about my hobbies; I asked about their play facilities. That was how it went until Claudia came back, and then this woman shook my hand very firmly and said—so *help* me—'Don't call us, we'll call you.' And they sure did. Claudia was rejected.

"No reasons. They never give you any reasons. You can't *imagine* how it feels—here you've gone through medical school and your wife was a philosophy major, and you both got honors—and your three-year-old kid is turned down by a nursery school."

The Interview has become so commonplace on the contemporary educational scene that children take it as a matter of course. "I can't come over to your house," one tells another. "I have an interview today." A family seeking a private school haven for two sons—one in the first grade and one in the fourth—reports that the elder was considerably miffed by what he saw as an intolerable advantage in his brother's appointment calendar. "Gee whiz," he told his mother, "Mike is going for his interview in the morning and missing school. Why can't I have any morning interviews? All mine are in the afternoon."

The Interview over, and the pupil—if he is one of that select minority upon whom fortune and the school psychiatrist have chosen to smile—safely ensconced in a private school, what is he likely to encounter? A closer look at this bastion of tomorrow's Ivy Leaguers seems in order.

The school we enter is large, lively, highly desirable, and charges, in the nursery years (it goes up later, and steeply), about $600 tuition, exclusive of school cap, midmorning milk, transportation, and the fund-raising drive among parents. It is one of the "professionally democratic" ilk, much given to psychiatric ponderings and theoretically moderate permissiveness, and utterly devoted to the concepts of Group Learning and Group Adjustment. (It was here that a visiting mother had the following harrowing experience: "Up on the top floor I saw a little boy, about a three-year-old, sitting on the steps, all alone, with his coat and muffler on, crying fit to break your heart and trying to put on his galoshes. I was so upset by the sight that I went looking for the teacher. Finally I found her in a classroom way down the hall and I said, 'Do you know there's a little boy sitting on the steps with his coat on, crying?' She turned purple, they always do when they think you're presuming to criticize them, and she said: 'Oh, yes, that's Billy. It's quite all right. He still hasn't learned how to put on his galoshes with the group.' ")

One enters the building shortly before nine A.M. and takes the elevator to the nursery school floor. Some fifty fathers having deposited their offspring ("Don't the mothers ever bring the children?" a teacher is asked, and she says, "Well, it's easier if the fathers do. The mothers may have younger children to take care of, or work to do at home, but the fathers can just drop them off on the way to the office"), the children disappear into a series of small rooms, where they settle down to work. There is a sandpile here, a water pumping-and-siphoning system there, desks and fingerpaints, rudimentary erector sets, and, somewhere along the line, a room for clay-working where, as the guide enthusiastically reports, every child can pop his creation into the "lit-tle kiln."

For a time, quiet reigns in the corridor. Then, suddenly, bedlam. Some twenty children are marching up and down the hall, wearing an odd assortment of headgear, banging miscellaneous objects made mostly of tin, and screaming, every one. "What are they doing?" the guide is asked. "Why, they're *wandering*," she says (you silly, what else would they be doing?). "In this period the hall belongs to them." What about discipline? she is asked. For example, if one child hit another, what would the teachers do? "We would try to preoccupy him with something else," she says. "We aim at helping them achieve *self*-disipline." And what, one asks, is that child there —the one who is lying on the floor making his eyes pop—what is *he* doing? "Who knows?" she says, with a gentle smile. "Perhaps he is thinking."

In one room on another floor, a first-grade music class is in session. The youngsters are barefoot, prancing around the floor, occasionally punching one another. One boy, banging a bongo drum in the center of the floor, is quite carried away; he is, the guide says, developing a sense of rhythm. In a doorway, the following conversation is overheard: Teacher: "Now go downstairs and get your book." Pupil: "No." Teacher: "Now." Pupil: "No." She shrugs helplessly and re-enters the room; he follows.

Next door, a "discussion group" is underway. "We believe in the fact that education is discussion within a group," the teacher says. "The children may talk about anything they want. We are talking now, for example, about the care of kittens. We believe in the freeing of the individual to his greatest creative capacity."

Sometimes the teacher asks a question. If a child volunteers the wrong answer, there is much lightness and gaiety, much gentle laughter from the teacher, much rumpling of his hair; no dunce's corner here. A decidedly informal tone prevails; if a child must be excused, there is no show of hands; he simply takes off. No bell marks the end of classes. The teacher simply says, "Okay, people," and they scoot out. It is all very adult.

"We want them to develop poise," says the head of the nursery school. "But do not think that we still follow the old ultra-progressiveness. Oh, no. In the old days you were so busy expressing yourself that others suffered in the process. Here our children have respect for their classmates, not because of the threat of discipline, but because of the threat of being ostracized. It becomes a matter of control by the group."

To illustrate group control at its most effective, she relates the story of Dougie. Dougie, it seems, began to act up in class, hitting other children, demanding his way, and otherwise making himself socially undesirable. The children began to knock Dougie around a bit to show their disapproval of his aggressive, maladjusted, antisocial behavior. And so one day, sensing trouble in the making, the teacher put her arm around Dougie and said to the group: "None of you are too happy with Dougie lately, are you?" No, they said. "Well, now," she said, hugging Dougie closer, "would you like to know why Dougie has been acting this way?" Yes, they said, and crowded around as for a bedtime story, while the teacher told them how Dougie had been having a lot of trouble at home of late; how his daddy had left the house and his mommy was not feeling well and the maid was being most unfriendly and Dougie did not feel loved. "Now," she said to her enraptured audience, "what do you think of that? What should Dougie do?" Whereupon these three- and four-year-olds embarked upon what was for all practical purposes a good, soul-satisfying group therapy session, and Dougie was restored to group grace.

"You would be amazed," concludes the nursery school lady, "at how understanding these children can be. All you have to do is *tell* them."

In a super-deluxe girls' school that has, some say, no greater glory than its past, the tactics are somewhat different.

From the moment one bangs a handsome, painfully well-polished brass knocker and a maid, attired in full white-apron regalia, opens the door, one senses an atmosphere of muted, almost muffled propriety. A group of pre-teen-agers, dressed in gym bloomers, comes around a corner, giggling a trifle loudly. From somewhere, perhaps from a passing teacher or even from one of the maids, comes a soft "sh!" and there is instant silence. A child bumps into the visitor and begs pardon with a graciousness quite frightening in one so young.

Teachers sweep by silently, smiling. On the bulletin board are notices of upcoming cultural events in town: operas, arty plays, ballets, concerts. One notice advertises a local production of a theater classic, and below is printed: "Girls! An exciting and important play for you to see!" The atmosphere, apparently, is infectious: as two maids scurry by, one is overheard saying to the other: "I heard him do Don Giovanni last week. He was divine . . ."

Finally the visitor is ushered into the office of the headmistress. "Our character," she says, "is friendliness and a stress on human values. The school always remains a part of our being, our family. We have no P.T.A.; we don't need one because we're all so close. Parents are welcome here all the time. Of course, a majority of the children are those of alumnae, but we try as much as possible to make room for suitable newcomers." What percentage of the 350 students are children and siblings of alumnae? Could it be, as has been estimated elsewhere, as high as 90 per cent? She doesn't know, the figures are not available; but, she points out gently, "We have, of course, a larger body of alumnae as we grow older. You understand, we must give preference to those who are our own, so to speak.

"Every child who comes here to be tested gets a plant cutting from our greenhouse, whether she's accepted or not, so that she will remember us. That is indicative of our friendliness and human touch.

"We have prayers for the whole school every morning. The teachers and children all lunch together. It is nice, very nice. We never took up the Dewey concept. We stuck to individual classes, in history, in geography and so forth. And there does seem to be"—with pride of vindication—"a trend back in that direction, doesn't there? Our older girls may choose electives. Russian was offered"—hesitantly, as reluctant proof of the school's progressive nature—"but no one elected it." (A small smile of relief.) "Yes, we do have a staff psychiatrist"—most cautiously, now—"but we prefer to call her a psychologist. We have a Drama Club, an Art Club, a Choral Group, a Current Events Club, a Fine Arts Club, a Dance Club, and a Junior Audubon Club. We still bird-watch in the park." (Happily; *that* will take the curse off those Russian courses any day.) "Every girl who graduates has a plan for further education, and we are proud that they *all get accepted in the college of their choice.*" Aye, there's the nub.

While not all the tradition-minded schools still bird-watch, each cultivates its own niceties. One has the students play recorders in grades three through seven. In another, the morning hymn is sung in French once a week. All of them have frequent lecturers—"They come and talk to the pupils about Bryn Mawr, Arabia, and welfare work." And almost all send their girl students to volunteer in some form of community or charity effort, as the rich have done with their daughters at least since the time of Louisa May Alcott's indestructibly altruistic *Rose in Bloom.*

The private schools have yet another point in common; it is significant and it surely, in these times, distinguishes them most sharply from the public schools: they can tell the interfering parent to go to blazes. If the parent takes umbrage, no matter; a hundred others are knocking at the door.

The private school, because it is well bred, is nice to parents. It invites them to drop in (by appointment) at any time, greets them with a smile, most graciously discusses any problem, and grants any reasonable request. But its *modus operandi* is Hands Off.

For child-centered parents, kin to those militant ranks of the P.T.A., it takes tremendous restraint to comply. But for the chance to see their child loved and respected by his peers, exquisitely adjusted to his world, skilled at a dinner party, splendid on a dance floor, well-endowed with the academic graces, including conversational French, and, most important, headed for Harvard, parents will make the ultimate sacrifice: They will shut up and, as one never says in the better private schools, butt out.

IN HEALTH

Pity the Pediatrician

Surely one of the noblest victims of our child-worshiping times is the pediatrician—an earnest man, a weary man, a man plagued in spades by time and awful circumstance.

Every now and again, in one of those sober-sided journals that circulate behind the scenes of medicine, comes a report on the Plight of the Pediatrician. There he stands, dedicated to a noble art and trained, long and laboriously, to treat the rare and exotic diseases of childhood. And here he crouches, a mere shadow of his once-sturdy self: reduced to a hand-holder, a telephone-answering service, a one-man well-baby clinic whose most awesome professional challenge, now that vaccines control most of the exotic ailments, is the care and pacification of Mother.

Pediatricians are the unhappiest men in the medical profession—and there are statistics to prove it. A survey taken by the magazine *Medical Economics* revealed that more pediatricians wish they were in some other specialty than men in any other branch of medicine. Some 37 per cent lament their calling (highest on the contentment scale, for reasons best known to themselves but not unfathomable to the rest of us, are psychiatrists).

"To enjoy pediatrics," said one of the principals interviewed in the survey, "you've got to love medicine and be crazy about children. Otherwise, you wouldn't be able to put up with the things their mothers do to you."

"Mother" was, in fact, the explanation most cited by pediatricians for what is getting them down. What do mothers do to them? They listed three chief complaints:

1. A preponderance of overanxious mothers has burdened the pediatrician with unnecessary telephone calls and house calls, and his presence is never more urgently requested than when he is home asleep.

2. The pediatrician often is not regarded as a skilled specialist, because so much of the service he gives (a full 90 per cent for coughs and colds) is routine. "You've really had it," one man pointed out, "when the anxious mother looks at you and says, 'Do you think Joey's sick enough to call in a regular doctor?'"

3. His hours are dismally long, and his remuneration is relatively low. He sees more patients, works harder, and has more irregular hours than any other doctor in his community, one pediatrician reported, "to produce an income lower than that of most local G.P.'s."

Take the matter of the telephone. Mothers call him on a staggering variety of such vital matters as, to glean one recent random sampling:

"Can I take Tommy to the beach with 103 temperature?"

"I am taking the baby to visit my mother in New Jersey

tomorrow and she is not used to the drinking water there. Should I bring some with me in a sterilized jar?"

"Can I send the boys out without sweaters tomorrow if tomorrow is warmer than today?"

"I was making whipped cream for the children and a mosquito fell in. Is it contaminated?" (A man with guts, this pediatrician ventured to inquire: "Why didn't you call the Health Department?" "Why should I?" the lady shot back. "*You're* the doctor.")

These doctors report an around-the-clock average of fifty to eighty calls, only a fraction of which—less than one-tenth, as a rule—concern sick children. A full three hours of office time may be taken up by the telephone, while hordes of restless tots pile up in the waiting room and mothers sit, vowing to switch to a man who will give them faster service. (They do, too.) Moreover, three hours of telephone talk means three hours of free consultation. "I had this woman calling from a pay station," one doctor recalls, "but I was on another line so she had to wait. When I finally got to her she was hopping mad because she'd waited twenty cents' worth. I told her, 'Okay, I'll deduct it from the bill I'll send you for this call.' I never saw her again."

There's the rub. Independence is a luxury the average pediatrician can ill afford, because pediatric customers are not egregiously loyal. In most communities there are fads in pediatricians; the skills and personality of a given man are a prime topic of conversation over the coffee cups. "A new man catches on with a circle of mothers," explains a pediatrician, "and he's got it made. As long as he can give each one plenty of time and sympathy and remember the children's symptoms and the mothers' first names, he will keep packing them in. But let him get busy, let him keep one mother and her child cooling their heels in the waiting room because six other women overstayed by ten minutes each, let him refuse to cover one night call for a baby with a rash on his belly, let him say to one woman, 'Let's see, now, which of your children was it who had the earache last month?'—and the fad dies down fast. The talk gets around that he's grown too 'independent,' and the pack jilts him.

"You've *got* to take those house calls and do all the rest of it, because if you don't someone else will. A mother will accept less service for herself; she'll hold off till morning to make an office visit if she doesn't feel well, and she'll forgive you if you don't know right away what's wrong with her. You can do anything with an adult, but when it comes to her child she's a howling fury. If that belly rash isn't as crucial to you as it is to her, heaven help you; you'll make out better selling shoes."

The pediatrician's dilemma is solidly underscored by a study —in depth, as they say—made by a prominent motivational research firm given to dispassionate analyses of all sorts of phenomena on the contemporary scene. The study is based on material culled from thousands of interviews with mothers, fathers, pediatricians, and G.P.'s.

Asking what women sought in their pediatricians, the researchers quoted typical answers given by the mothers and then ferreted out their true feelings. For example: A woman says, "My pediatrician should be easily available, conveniently located, call back in no more than an hour or two." Her deeper meaning, according to the research team, is that the doctor should be ready, double-parked and motor running, so to speak, to rush to her home at all times, and willing to talk to her on the telephone at any hour.

Or she says, "He should be patient, unhurried." Her deeper

meaning: She wants to be treated as if she and her offspring are the doctor's only patients, and fie on those hordes in the waiting room.

Again, the lady says: "I want to be remembered. He should call us by our first names." What she means Down Deep, the researchers say, is that she and her bairn should be so totally unique to the medical man that he finds himself thinking of them even when he hasn't seen them for months.

And finally: "He should be devoted and like children." Her deeper meaning: "He should practice medicine for the love of it. . . . He should never be too busy, and when his schedule begins to be crowded, should refuse to accept new patients for a time. Of course, I expect him to be crazy about children and to have a bunch of his own. And he should give me the feeling that he won't ever put me off for a good game of golf."

It takes no oversensitive ear to detect in much of the above the loud, clear ring of a woman talking about her analyst. It is a tone fraught with love, hostility, petulance, possessiveness, unreasoning demand. Dentists almost never hear it; nor do orthopedists, or radiologists, or EENT men. But the pediatrician knows it well. Since he is dealing with the *child,* crass monetary considerations should be beyond his ken; he should be able to speak, with feeling, of *"my* children," *"my* mothers" —a pair of Small Touches that are *de rigueur* in this business —and he should be able to commit to memory (reading the charts in front of mothers is dirty pool) the name, age, fears, foibles, and general state of every tot. If he can remember the same of mother, so much the better.

Confronted with such sentiments and much, much more in a similar vein, the motivational researchers saw fit to draw a conclusion: The pediatrician seemed, they said, to be uneasy and uncertain about just what sort of doctor he was supposed to be. "He seems to be frustrated by what he good-humoredly refers to as his 'hand-holding function.' . . . And yet it is this hand-holding function, knowingly and systematically extended to all areas of doctor-baby-mother-husband-family relationships, which could assure the pediatrician a new and definite role in the life of the family and in our society."

Positive thinking, this; but try telling it to the doctor. He just doesn't enjoy holding hands. He knows that reassurance and anticipatory medicine ("At ten to twelve months the baby will start showing a loss of appetite; don't worry, it's perfectly normal.") are an essential part of pediatrics, and he is, of course, all for them. But the routine stuff is almost all he has, since many mothers patronize him for the check-ups and shots and general advice on the care, feeding, and emotional well-being of the young, but turn to the family man (the "regular doctor") when real illness strikes. Lads fresh out of medical school, whose training has been weighted heavily toward well-baby care, may accept—good-humoredly or not—their hand-holding function. But for the man who's been around a time, this is a far, far more bitter pill to swallow than any he ever prescribes.

Such being the case, why go into pediatrics? "Because you don't know what you're getting into," says one unhappy fellow. He explains that the intern's introduction to the specialty is through hospital pediatrics and clinic cases. Parents who bring their child to a clinic, he says, are not generally the sort to worry because he doesn't sleep well. "When you're struggling to make ends meet, who's got the time or energy to worry about a poor sleeper? These people bring their child in when he's really *sick*. But the people who lead soft, cushy lives —the middle-class people I see in my office—they're bothered by smaller things. They get all wrought up about nail-biters and bed-wetters.

"Fifteen years ago, on the pediatric wards, I saw exciting

cases, challenging cases, and I thought private practice would be just like that. But I was living in a dream world. Private practice is exhaustive and abrasive and dull. I see fifty to sixty patients a day, and most of them have nothing wrong except that they're spoiled. I spend every day listening to unbelievable noise and physically wrestling with hostile children—and for *what?*"

Further, the question develops, for *whom?* "If I could just slip the mother a happy pill and tell her to leave the child alone, I'd be fine," says one practitioner. "But you can't do that. So many of these mamas once studied a little psychology and they never got over it. They are ridden—ridden!—with guilt that possibly they aren't being as good mothers as they should. So they badger us with inane questions about child development and they bring us their perfectly healthy kids to satisfy their own neurotic needs for reassurance.

"The allergists are kept busy with this kind of thing, too. In the old days mothers used to say, 'The kid has the sniffles.' But nowadays they haul them to dozens of specialists—'Smell the grass, smell the wool.' In my experience the children pediatricians and allergists see most of are the rejected children. They are full of psychosomatic ailments and the mothers keep dragging them around to doctors to assuage their own guilt."

(Somewhat tangential, but not altogether dissociated, is the matter of orthodontia, a flourishing trade. In earlier days orthodontic work was a primarily cosmetic venture designed for the embellishment of rich men's daughters. Today it is, of course, a recognized investment in the future health of a tot's teeth. Nonetheless, when pressed, orthodontists will suggest some other reasons for their own current popularity:

1. Orthodontia is the thing to do. Among nine- to twelve-year-old girls, particularly, says one doctor, braces are a mark

of belonging, and many a girl child who doesn't urgently need them actually expresses disappointment, because most of her friends have them.

2. It is a sort of status symbol. The appliances in a child's mouth bespeaks his parents' affluence, since the bill for this kind of work generally runs in excess of $1,000.

3. It shows that parents *care.* "Extensive orthodontia is not essential for every one of my patients," says one of these men. "But you take a mother who feels a little guilty to begin with, because she is paying too much for her own clothes or spending too much time on the golf course, or feels tied down by her child, or whatever. Putting $1,200 or $1,500 into the child's mouth makes her feel better, and it doesn't do the child any harm.")

If the overanxious mother makes life difficult for the pediatrician when her child is well, she can make it absolutely miserable when the child is really sick. Just ask any nurse on the pediatric floor of any hospital.

"Oh, it's just awful to see how these women have our doctors intimidated," says one hardy creature who bears the scars of fourteen years' service as the head pediatric nurse in a large suburban hospital. "For instance, we have strict rules here about visiting hours, but the doctors won't enforce them. They're scared to. *We* have to. Then we can take the blame and they can pacify the parents."

Strolling down a pediatric corridor as she speaks, she pauses at the doorway of a room. "Now, here's a little boy with the shingles. His mother insisted that we put a cot in his room and let her stay all night. Every time the boy made a noise she came running out like a wild woman, looking for a nurse. She was such a pest that none of us had any peace, including the patient. The next day we told the doctor, and he agreed she had to go. But he wouldn't tell her himself. He asked us to.

"Here [at the next doorway] is a child who had major surgery to correct a large bowel. Ever since, he's been holding back on using the bedpan because he was scared he might hurt himself. So the parents made a bargain with him. They would come in every day and stay all day, playing cards with him, on condition that he would use the bedpan. When they were ready to leave he'd throw a tantrum and threaten to go back on the bargain, so they'd panic and stay some more. They were practically living here, and the child was becoming a real tyrant. Finally we kicked them out and took away the cards and told him there'd be no more bargains no matter *what*. He's been fine ever since.

"Now, here . . . This one had to have a little ear operation, nothing much, and the mother promised him, 'I'll be there when you wake up.' She couldn't be there when the child woke up, because that would be in the recovery room and it's strictly against the rules. When we told her, she said, 'But I've *got* to be. I *promised!* What will happen to him *psychologically?*'

"Well, we stood firm, and she went all the way up to the director, who told her either to go home and not come back till visiting hours or to take the child out and take the responsibility herself. Finally she left. I'll tell you what happened to that child psychologically: He is more relaxed than he's been in years because his mother isn't on his neck all the time."

But what wears down the pediatrician even more than the hospital demeanor of some mothers is the urge of many more to compare. More succinctly, to compete. One of the ten most frequent complaints of pediatricians mentioned in that motivational research report is that mothers often use their children to joust with other mothers. The yardstick is the child next door, or a cousin's or best friend's baby. Is her offspring less vocal at X years than the X-aged specimen next door? Tell the doctor. Less of a bully [euphemism: healthy aggression]? Tell the doctor. Less advanced in height, weight, eating habits, toilet habits, sleeping habits, playing and learning habits than that next-door paragon? Tell, oh tell the doctor. "They get worried when their own children don't forge ahead of the neighbor's children," one says. "They aren't really worried about the *children,* you see, but they're afraid maybe they don't look as good as the mothers next door, and that burns them. If your kids aren't keeping up with the Joneses' kids, doesn't it follow that you're not keeping up with the Joneses?"

This anxiety seems to be particularly virulent in the densely mined fields of toilet training. A woman who is having no luck with her offspring may, doctors say, become supremely dejected in the face of a housebreaking next door. And even after success is won, she compares. One woman called her pediatrician with the alarming intelligence that, whereas the neighbor's child was using the potty four times a day, hers used it only three. What was wrong with her child? "The worst of it," this man says, "was that in some subtle, screwy way, she blamed me. They always do." Then there was the stunned pediatrician to whom a woman confided her fearful suspicion that her son did not masturbate at an age when, by consensus of her friends and acquaintances, he should. Question: Should he be encouraged?—and, if so, how?

This leads to another familiar type: the consulter. She is a mother who, simply, consults, with anyone who will listen, on the methods and manners of child care. She will lend an ear to the opinions of strange women in the park, men behind pharmaceutical counters, second cousins of other doctors, and bear this body of expertise into the pediatrician's office to fling, like a glove, into his face. (One survey indicates that, excluding the doctor, a mother gets 43 per cent of her information regarding child care from friends, neighbors, and other mothers; 33 per cent of it from Dr. Spock, really more of an institution than a pediatrician, and one that will be taken up shortly, and 23 per cent from other miscellaneous sources. That leaves 1 per cent. It belongs to husbands, and no one can take it away from them.)

"The consulter is usually a woman who shops pediatricians," one victim complains. "She lugs her child around to one after another, seeking the man who will tell her what she wants to hear." Typically, the pediatrician-shopper leaves her current man abruptly, without warning or explanation; half the time he hasn't the vaguest idea why and it would, of course, be most impolitic for him to ask. But several mothers, all staunch pediatrician-shoppers, recently supplied some answers:

"Well, he was a good doctor, I never doubted that [this is a standard opener; pediatricians are almost never condemned on purely medical grounds], but he would always keep me waiting. One day I complained about it and he said, 'Listen, I'm dealing with people, not piecework, and you'll have to wait your turn. Other people have children too.' I didn't think *that* was a very good attitude, so I left."

"I know he took good care of the children, but I got the feeling we weren't really important to him. For instance, I'd hear him call other mothers by their first names, but he never did me. And sometimes he even forgot the children's names and I'd have to remind him. Well, if we were *important* to him, wouldn't he at least remember our names?"

"My girl friends were all raving about this new man, so I decided to try him, that's all. I wouldn't say he's any better than our old pediatrician, but he does intuit children beautifully."

And inevitably: "I was having serious disciplinary problems with my daughter, and I asked the pediatrician to help. All he ever did was talk to her once, and then he referred me to a child guidance counselor. Can you imagine?"

Yes, indeed. But while this man ducked—and lost a patient —it is a hard fact of the pediatrician's life that he himself often must play counselor, a job for which he has little training, little time and, alas, less reimbursement. "When I see a woman and her children periodically for, say, fourteen or fifteen years," says one man, "I am more than a family doctor. I am a member of the family, and she expects all kinds of services for free. Say a child has a psychiatric problem. The parents take him to a psychiatrist and it does no good. So they come to me (and when a mother and father show up together in my office, I can expect real trouble). They say, 'If you would only talk to the boy and guide us a little. You *know* him. You've known us all for years. What does the psychiatrist know about us? Only *you* can help.' That's the trap you're caught in. It isn't really part of the job, but you have to do it— talk and listen, and struggle with their complaints and family tensions—all this for five dollars a visit, while the psychiatrist is making twenty-five.

"Or you get special problems. . . . Right now I've got this woman who's getting a divorce, and she's kept me on the telephone a half hour a day for the past week, crying about how will she break it to the children and how can I help so they won't be traumatized. . . . And then her husband gets me on the phone and starts in the same way. I sympathize with these people, but it's just too much. They wouldn't do it to anyone else except an analyst—and he wouldn't give them the telephone time."

Unlike his fellow sorely tried mortals, the pediatrician dare not even allow such burdens to age him before his time. For pediatricians cannot grow old. It is an unhappy axiom of the trade that mothers prefer to patronize their own contemporaries. The younger man is "more up on things," has "more psychiatric orientation," has "a more modern point of view."

Since his patients remain within a fairly constant age group, the pediatrician is one of the few men in medicine (others: obstetricians) who may find himself over the hill by middle age. An obstetrician can become a full-time gynecologist when he starts outgrowing his mothers, points out one cheerless fellow pushing forty-five, but what can the pediatrician become? "Poor."

There is a forty-year-old ex-pediatrician, widely celebrated in one New England metropolis, who got out while the getting was good. Two years ago, he quit practice and moved into his wife's family business. He is a European, who practiced in his native country for some years before coming here, and his observations on the comparison are illuminating.

"Where I come from," he begins dourly, "the pediatrician is a highly respected specialist, a man of standing. Here, he is a wet nurse. He is at the mercy of a mother who is desperate, and often unqualified, to be a good mother, and she, in turn, is at the mercy of her child. She demands custom care for this custom child and she can be quite ferocious if she doesn't get it.

"She doesn't really want the doctor to help her with her responsibilities, but to take them off her shoulders and ease her guilt while he does so. The middle-class girl in this country is the family pet, overindulged and overprotected. At nineteen or twenty she gets married, and a year later she has a baby. Hooray! In other countries it is a quite normal process but here it is a spectacular production. [It doesn't necessarily take a foreigner to strike this reproachful note. "The American middle class," Margaret Mead has said, with none of the vested jaundice of the pediatrician, "treats motherhood as a unique achievement."]

"While she is still in the hospital in her lace bed jacket her mother says, 'Don't worry about a thing, darling. You won't have to move. We will take care of everything.' And they do. She comes home from the hospital and a nurse moves right in with her. Then she lies recumbent for three weeks while her family coddles her and the nurse proceeds to make her completely incompetent. When I was in practice I always knew the first time my telephone would ring: it was the day the nurse left.

"The grandparents are around night and day. The husband acts as though she'd done him a splendid favor. I once had a new father who gave his wife a diamond ring. I said, 'What did you give her the ring for?' He looked at me, hurt. 'Well, after all,' he said, 'she has *given* me a *son!*'

"You don't get that sort of thing where I come from. Here a girl is pregnant and her parents wring their hands and say, 'How can she take care of a baby? She's still a baby herself.' There, they say, 'Wonderful. Now she is truly grown and she will be able to stand on her own two feet.'

"Then, those formulas. Infant feeding is a nightmare in this country. In my country everybody uses the same thing, it's a standard formula and any moron can mix it. But here they keep experimenting with fancier formulas for fancier babies. All this dreadful fuss and concern! And of course the children show it. I never had occasion to give a sedative to a child until I came here. In my country it is unheard-of. Here we are forever giving the youngsters 'fussy pills.' You have no *idea* the quantity of tranquillizers that are given to children in this country.

"I never had mothers constantly on the telephone back home. There are child health clinics and the mother with a routine problem talks to a pediatric nurse. But here—what mother will settle for a nurse? For *her child's* diarrhea, only a doctor will do.

"Pediatric practice in the United States is no way to enjoy

life. The pediatricians I know are hollow-eyed men with in-
cipient ulcers. Awful. So I decided to get out while there was
still time. It was the smartest thing I ever did."

Not every pediatrician, of course, has good business connec-
tions in the family, and so such success stories are rare. More
generally, the only way for a pediatrician to be happy is to be
a pediatrician without a practice. One method is to retreat to
Academia, where a man may enjoy the best of both worlds,
doing research or teaching in the field he theoretically loves,
yet insulated from mothers by walls of ivy. Another, and better still, is to become a pediatric celebrity, retiring from practice and dispensing professional advice to mothers from the
safe distance of a speakers' platform or a printed page. This
is a glorious solution, achieved by few men, and none more
notably than that most dazzling light in the pediatric galaxy,
Dr. Spock.

Benjamin McLane Spock recognized early that mothers
were a breed no man could fight alone, so he joined them.
In 1946 he wrote a book called, if there be those who don't
yet know, *The Common Sense Book of Baby and Child Care.*
It enjoyed something more than a modest success, and has
since become what his publishers claim is the biggest best-
seller ever published in this country, with the exception of the
Bible and miscellaneous works of Shakespeare, which have,
after all, a certain chronological edge.

In 1947 Spock quit private practice and moved on to the
good life: teaching, researching, speaking, appearing on television, writing magazine columns. Today he is, undoubtedly,
the only perambulating brand name in the business. His book
is almost never called by its proper title. Mothers commonly
refer to it as "Dr. Spock," or simply as "the bible." They tend
—even those who cannot be classed as full-time consulters—

to quote it at length to their own pediatricians, which can cause a certain professional strain.

A weary pediatric man recently cited as one of the occupational hazards that were driving him crazy, "sentences that begin, 'But Dr. Spock says . . .' I tell you, I am damn sick and tired of hearing what Dr. Spock says."

Why is the Spockian influence on motherhood so formidable?

Spockism offers reassurance. Most of the practicing fellows offer it too, of course; but they can hand it out only piecemeal, during office hours when other mothers are queueing up outside, or during house calls when they are tired and in a hurry, or during telephone conversations when they are, understandably, less concerned with comforting chit-chat than with getting the devil off the wire.

But Spockism, preserved on the printed page, offers reassurance twenty-four hours a day. Moreover, it devotes its total attention to the reader alone; it awaits no other woman in the outside office, it is never in a hurry, it is never short-tempered or brusque or accusing or out on a golf course, it is infinitely loving, tender, sympathetic, patient, and it never sends bills. Spockism gives to the modern mother, paddling about frantically in a dark pool of Freudian implications, torn between the embattled forces of Discipline and Permissiveness, dazed by the potential perils of rejection, affection, early weaning, late toilet-training, and chronic thumb-sucking, traumatized by the fear of causing a trauma and helplessly stuck with the suspicion that a little psychiatric orientation is a burdensome thing—to her, any time she needs it, Spockism gives surcease from anxiety, relief from guilt, the blessed assurance that the sun will rise tomorrow even if she should bow to her instincts and say tonight: "Beat it, you brat, you'll eat when I'm ready."

Warm comfort begins to envelop the mother at the very outset of the Spock epic. "You know more than you think you do," writes the doctor, in what by now must be the most widely known opening line since "Call me Ishmael." "Don't take too seriously all that the neighbors say. Don't be overawed by what the experts say. Don't be afraid to trust your own common sense." And he then continues, through 627 (hardcover) consistently friendly, tirelessly casual, exhaustively indexed pages ("Blueness: in breath-holding, 204; mottled skin, 198; from nitrates, 125"), to tell her all that she thinks she doesn't know.

"If Dr. Spock doesn't cover it," says one disciple, "it hasn't happened. He has an explanation for a bump over the left eyebrow at five o'clock in the evening." And another notes: "If your child puts beans up his nose you will find what to do in Spock and you probably will find it cross-indexed under 'beans' and under 'nose.' What you *won't* find is any Freudian mumbo-jumbo, and that is fine with me."

This last is not precisely true. There is much that is Freudian in Spock, because Spock is a Freudian-thinking man. He has simply mastered the trick, as few others have, of serving up Freudian concepts camouflaged in such palatable form that they slide like soda pop down the most distrustful gullet. "He makes Freud *folksy*," says one reader, and this makes almost everyone happy. For the mother who once took that course in Basic Psychology, it signals a kindred spirit; for the mother who didn't, it painlessly opens up whole new horizons.

Take, for example, the Spockian approach to the psychiatrically loaded question of why children sometimes get the idea that their parents are out to devour them. There stands Spock, up on a lecture platform, addressing—his approach varies little with his audience—colleagues, medical students, or the ladies of the P.T.A. He is fashioned along altogether vertical lines:

lanky and six feet four, a silhouette that encourages the illusion, despite the conservative precision of his dress, that his suit is a mite short in the sleeves and trouser legs. At the ends of those sleeves dangle a pair of exceedingly large hands, which he now flings out in a widespread purple gesture as he fixes a bright eye and a vast grin upon some imaginary tot in the audience and exclaims, in a loud rhapsody of affection: "You are as sweet as candy. I am going to EAT YOU UP!"

It is precisely this sort of thing that makes mothers feel Spock is a man who understands. Just what it is that he understands doesn't matter; he supports them against a critical world in general and critical experts in particular.

"Ben," says a friend from the early days of his practice, "gives status back to women. It's a revelation to see audience reaction to him. The women strain toward him, they're happy, they seem to be saying, 'Tell me more! Tell me again that I'm not so bad! Reassure me that it won't be awful if I get angry with my child! Tell me!' It is almost a form of group therapy."

His book elicits much the same response from women as his presence. They constantly send him long treatises upon their own maternal trials and triumphs, accompanied by pictures of their children, regards from their families, and best wishes to his. "I feel as though you're writing just for *me*," one typically notes. And another: "I cannot take any decision concerning my baby's development without consulting your book first, and I repeat every day and every moment to my friends and relatives, 'Dr. Spock says this, Dr. Spock says that. . . .' "

Being human, Spock is pleased; being dedicated, he is distressed. "When I have written a book expressly to make parents rely more on their own instincts, it is disconcerting to have a mother tell me that she keeps one copy in the living room, one in the bedroom, one in the bathroom, and is thinking of buying another for the upstairs hall.

"I remember," he continues, half in pleasure, half in pain, "addressing two thousand people in Chicago one day. And I got the feeling that if I were to stand in front of that microphone and say, 'Testing, 1, 2, 3, 4, testing, 1, 2, 3, 4,' they would have nodded to each other and said, 'How true, how true.'"

It should only happen to me, sighs the neighborhood pediatrician. And yet, how could it? Does Spock have to answer the telephone? Does Spock have to put up with consulters and competers? Does Spock have a mother sitting on the other side of the desk, seeing her own troubles mirrored in his eyes?

To Spock goes the glory; to the local pediatric man go the problem eaters and the problem nail-biters—and, of course, the problem mothers. Pity, indeed, the pediatrician: one of the nobler victims, largely unsung, of these child-worshiping times.

AFTER HOURS

The Coketail Party

The rebels rose in Westport, Connecticut. Rebels had risen in Westport before and surely would again, but never with more courage or for a less popular cause.

"PTA Asks an End to Dance Classes for Sixth-Graders," the headlines proclaimed. There followed reports that this brave band was lobbying for the abandonment of public-school dance classes for eleven-year-olds, which the P.T.A. itself had sponsored. "There seems to be a general trend these days to bring the social experience down further in the age scale," the P.T.A. president said, "and we hope to reverse the trend." Henceforth, if the P.T.A. won its good fight, the social experience would move back up the scale where it belonged: to the seventh grade. "The children are trying to grow up too fast," she added, apparently forgetting, in the fine flush of battle, who had started those classes.

But why remind her? Any number of P.T.A.'s have sponsored dance classes; and any number of P.T.A.'s in recent seasons have been grumbling—along with the educators, the psychologists, the family counselors—about the dazzling social precocity of the young. But the Westport mothers did not merely grumble. They acted; and that, in the face of the tide, took guts.

The tide is such that a manufacturer of stationery supplies saw nothing but sound business recently in bringing forth an appointment calendar designed exclusively for children. It came bound in pink for girls, blue (navy) for boys; bore, just after the frontispiece, a blank page for Telephone Numbers of My Friends; provided outsized space for the hours of every calendar day to accommodate third-grade penmanship, and at last report was, as the trade has it, moving nicely.

Of course it was; it filled a genuine need. How else is one to keep track of the after-school dates, the birthday parties, the bowling parties, the luncheon and—in some circles—the dinner parties, to say nothing of the coketail parties, currently the snappiest of them all? And the club meetings? And the benumbing roster of appointments in pursuit of gracious living: the guitar, piano, and recorder lessons, the dancing—Westport notwithstanding—lessons, the language lessons, the art lessons, the judo lessons and, in season, the swimming, riding, skiing, and tennis lessons? When one recalls that this social lion must also fit in his pediatrician, his orthodontist, his allergist, and, alas, not too rarely, his psychiatrist, the wonder is that he ever got along without an appointment book at all.

It has been suggested that what this superbly organized child needs more than anything else is time—time to sit alone under the apple tree and simply muse. The question is: Does he know how to sit alone and muse? And would he want to, even if he did? There still may be children around who putter in happy solitude with empty coffee cans or, in their livelier moments, crouch with the neighborhood aficionados over a smashing good game of marbles, but life's heady pace has broken most tykes of such quaint preoccupations; what *does* preoccupy them is summed up chillingly in the recent comment of one eleven-year-old en route to a party. "I don't expect to make out tonight," he said, "because I am shy."

The jargon of the social set is potent stuff. A fifth-grade girl, talking with a buddy on the telephone, sounds like a cagey post-deb making a date. "I don't know if I can see you tomorrow," she says. "I may be busy." Or: "I can't. I have dancing class tomorrow and my orthodontist Friday. Want to have lunch Saturday?"

A ten-year-old boy, asked why he has given up a longtime friend, explains: "Aw, Pete's always busy. He called me last week to come over to his house but I had plans to go bowling. So we tried to figure out a date and he was busy all week. So we made a date for the next week. So he was supposed to call me and he didn't, and I didn't because I thought *he* should, so he got mad. So I figured, You've had it, buddy. So then his mother gets into the act and calls *my* mother to find out why I never call Peter any more. Who needs him?"

Mothers in areas where the high life abounds report that wee ones commonly ask, "May I have a dinner date with Meg Saturday?" and "May I have a nighttime date with Meg?"— meaning, respectively, May I eat at Meg's house? and May I sleep at Meg's house? Real dinner parties are, if not yet commonplace, at least in high favor with the trend-setters. "When I gave one for my son's friends," says a mother, "I was more nervous than if my husband's boss was coming to dinner. It's foolish—but what can you do? Some mother who thought it was a cute idea started it and then all the other kids began nagging their parents to do the same. I put up a fight, but my boy said, 'Mother! Do you want my friends to feel rejected in this house?' I was licked."

With this surfeit of entertainments, small wonder the young have lost their taste for daisy-picking and other forms of prop-free fun. "My daughter and her friends plan days in advance for an after-school date," a parent says. "The phone calls go back and forth till I could scream. Finally they fix the day and the hour—just when I'm supposed to be downtown. But my child says, 'Oh, Mommy, if the girls can't come over I'll just *die*. It's all *arranged* and everything.' So I switch my own date, and the other mothers ferry their girls to our house, and then what happens? These kids sit around for hours and wonder what there is to *do*."

Ah, what *is* there to do? In this long, pale winter of his discontent, jaded even beyond the pleasures of his personal TV set, the child seeks restlessly, not unlike the International Set yachting in the same old waters, for some new sensation. And mothers strive manfully to provide it.

One way is the birthday party, an institution which in recent years has been shaken to its core. Gone the musical chairs. Gone the donkey's tail, the cake and ice cream and the little paper baskets filled with candy from the five-and-dime. Today, any self-respecting party has a Theme; the swinging affair has hired entertainment, and the *succès fou* has a caterer—who is nowadays not a caterer at all, but a Specialist in Children's Parties.

The resultant soirée has been aptly described in a straight *New York Times* report on trends in children's parties. The story quoted a woman who was present when her grandson and ten guests gathered to make merry on the occasion of his fifth birthday:

"What impressed her most, the grandmother said, was not the professional puppet show, but the food. There were gaily decorated small sandwiches cut into crescents, circles, and squares, and the caterer had filled them with such tea-party spreads as tuna fish salad, shrimp salad, and chicken salad. . . . Actually, such fare is simple when compared to the individual bacon, caviar, or mushroom omelets another caterer creates for young people's parties. This caterer, whose parties for 60 to 150 children can cost up to $500, says six-year-olds prefer 'tiny jelly omelets,' and that he has had requests for truffles." (For one mother, a gourmet cook whose children expect the best, the problem is heightened. Scorning caterers, she turned out a gorgeous table for her daughter's ninth birthday, and the small one said: "Oh, mother. Not truffles again.")

Standard entertainment at such affairs is a magician, a clown, or a puppeteer. But newer and better is the Children's Party Coordinator, a combination baby-sitter and visiting social director. A coordinator, as one of the breed explains, is superior to a clown because he guides the children into making their *own* fun, which is constructive. But then, let the man tell it his way:

"I do not entertain. I am a Party Fun Leader. It isn't always a birthday. I do Valentine's Day parties and Fourth of July parties and first boy-and-girl get-togethers—those are very popular for the older children, nine or ten. But the formula is always the same: We have fun by sharing the fun experience with our friends. Norman Vincent Peale says that the best way to relax is to laugh and sing, and that is just what we do. I have a guitar and a large file of games. First the children eat and then we sing and play. We have a theme. Like, if it's a birthday that comes around election time we have a political theme: Vote for Joseph, He's the Best. It is a complete participation program. The games are so great even the grown-ups love them. It is what I call a lot of intelligent hilarity.

"I have been booked into very successful parties for three-year-olds. You'd be surprised what good party people three-year-olds can be when you guide them right. There is a maturation process that takes place in them between the time I arrive and the time I leave."

Children's Party Fun Leaders charge from $25 ("for a little home gathering") to upwards of $50 for large, splendidly catered affairs. They are a relatively new breed of specialist, and they were born successful. Why? "Because the parents can't cope with twenty-five or thirty kids, that's why," another practitioner says. "They have enough trouble coping with their own. I go into a house, the mother is a wreck. She says, 'Thank God you're here.' I hear that all the time. They're deadly scared to let me leave until the last kid is gone. I did one party where I never even saw the mother until it was over. She said to me, 'You were marvelous. The party was wonderful.' I said, 'How do you know? You weren't even there.' She said, 'That's why it was wonderful.' "

Like many of his associates, this man considers the caterer expendable. "It's a crime, all that money. 'Give 'em a Coke and a hot dog,' I tell the mothers. 'The kids don't eat all that fancy stuff.' But they still order it. They tell me the kids *will* eat it, but I see a hell of a lot of cheese tarts left over for the dog. Personally I think the mother gets satisfaction out of complaining to people that she had to spend $200 for her child's birthday party."

A correspondent from Hollywood, where climate and budget permit, reports that all the better birthday parties are held under the Big Tent on one's own grounds. Herself a producer's wife with three children, she has been under a lot of tents, and most vividly recalls one that housed a latter-day C. B. DeMille production: star, supporting cast of 80-odd, 120 extras—the parents—plus caterers, musicians, cowboys, ponies, magician, clown, ventriloquist, and M.C. (The sweetest touch of all, as she tells it, was one of the guests—a famous TV and film comedian who accompanied his two daughters and, whenever he thought no one was peeking, whipped out a pocket comb and tidied up their bangs.)

But such galas, after all, require taste and money. For mothers who want to make a big splash but can't foot the bill, it is much more difficult. Many devote extraordinary amounts of time and energy to dreaming up new and imaginative menus and Themes, and considering their handicap they succeed brilliantly. Among the parties recently served up in several communities: a nightclub motif for a ten-year-old birthday child, wherein the guests, male and female, danced under dimmed lights and soda pop was served out of champagne bottles; an Oriental party for nine-year-olds, attended in costume and illuminated by Japanese lanterns, the menu featuring egg roll and lobster Cantonese; a cowboy party for boys only, at which the cake was shaped like a covered wagon ("I *tried* to get a chocolate horse put on, too," said the mother, "but the cost was prohibitive"), and a pony dropped in to trot each guest around the front lawn; a tramp party, at which the food was served in tin cans with the rough edges filed down; a "Come as your mother" party, at which the costume-prize winner showed up with curlers and cold cream, causing her parent a certain discomfort; and a ballerina party, for which the guests were adorned in leotards, the birthday girl wore a tiara and the cake was a ballerina, a wondrous creation with golden hair and silver sprinkles on a pink tutu.

"What a time we had!" says the mother who masterminded this final caper. "I stayed up every night for a week planning the details. The morning of the party, the cake came. It was awful. The hair was dyed green and the cake had a lump in the middle so the ballerina looked pregnant. I had to take it back to the bakery, between delivering one kid to a music lesson and another to a Brownie meeting and finding a sitter for the baby. And the party decorations still weren't done, or anything. In one hour I set the table, made a crepe-paper canopy, got the Degas reproductions up on the walls, picked up the kids and brought them home and finished making my daughter's tiara. It turned out to be a lovely party and the mothers still haven't stopped calling to congratulate me on the ballerina cake. But good heavens, never again!"

Nonsense.

A relatively recent innovation is the birthday party *out:* the bowling party, the movie party, the luncheon party. Membership in a country club is particularly helpful here. Maître d's interviewed in several smart restaurants report that birthday luncheons for five-year-olds are not uncommon. "But the food is usually simple, like hamburgers," says one. "The idea is so outrageous to begin with that I guess these mothers don't have the nerve to pour it on with a fancy menu, too."

But the toddler birthday parties—they are even given for infants of one—are the real tip-off. A mother who puts forth a sumptuously decorated table, racks her brains for amusing party favors, and dresses her two-year-old birthday boy in his most splendid raiment can hardly pretend, even to herself, to be doing it for the child's benefit.

One stalwart abstainer puts it square on the line. "It is a form of competitiveness among the mothers. Just like adult dinner parties. These gals knock themselves out thinking up original gimmicks and planning their kids' costumes. My sister-in-law pulled a real coup: she had a birthday cake made like a gingerbread house. Every time I came over, for weeks before the party, she'd be practicing, putting layers of a gingerbread house into the oven or taking them out. The cake was a triumph and all the kids' mothers told her how clever it was. That's how she gets her kicks.

"Well, who are they doing all this for—the kids? The kids don't know the difference and couldn't care less. They wouldn't give a hoot if you filled the bathtub with ice cream and let them wade in. In fact, they'd love it.

"It's the same thing with birthday gifts. I can remember when the going price for a gift was one dollar. Now it's become really embarrassing. At my daughter's parties the children bring presents worth seven and eight dollars, and then of course we have to return the courtesy. For one party I bought a five-dollar blouse and my daughter said, 'Oh, Mom, it just won't do. It's cute, but it's not as *smart* as the one Barbara brought me.' I think the whole thing is immoral, but how can my child be the only one who shows up with a coloring book?"

Thus inspired, the kids themselves develop a marvelously mature flair for high living. A group of eleven-year-olds recently booked an eight-way conference call to extend birthday felicitations and congratulations to a sixth-grade colleague. A ten-year-old girl took it upon herself to call a dance studio and arrange for a professional team to come teach her coketail party guests—a backward group, apparently—how to cha-cha. Her parents scolded, but made no discernible effort to keep the story under their hats; by gum, kid's got initiative. A nine-year-old boy turned down a party invitation and told his mother, "I'm tired of that crowd." When he turned down a second, and a third, she became worried about possible anti-social tendencies and asked ("gently, so he wouldn't think I was intruding,") what was wrong. *"Nothing* is wrong," he said, "but when you've been to one you've been to them all."

In this ambience a parent whose child is slow is naturally worried. "My son had his first heterosexual date today," a mother reported. "I'm so *happy*. He is very small for his age and I was afraid he would be backward socially." How old was this redeemed runt? "Eleven," she said.

There are parents who like to see little boys and girls together because they look, as they say, adorable. There are others who have their doubts, but seek solace in nostalgic musings. One mother said recently, "They're not really so much more precocious than we were. It just seems that way. I can remember when I was eleven we went to boy-girl parties and played post office." And turning to her own eleven-year-old, she asked, "Are you kids playing post office yet?" No, the child said. "Spin the bottle?" No. "Any kissing games at all?" "Oh, we have kissing," said the blushing babe, "but my goodness, Mother, it's *not games.*"

Whither now? All manner of experts are quite beside themselves with concern about the effect of social pressures on the young. Fortunately they aren't just talking about it. They are doing something about it: they are investigating it. One study, reported at a conference of the Eastern Psychological Association in New York, tried to determine whether the high incidence of neurotic behavior in a group of youngsters age three to six was due in any part to parental pressure for premature social achievement. The group came from middle-class families moving upward in the social scale. The parents were all either professional or planning professional careers and, to a one, held "communication and early socialization" vitally important. They all strove to give their children "every early advantage," notably dancing and music lessons, and many reported encouraging parties *and dating;* although what constitutes a date in the three-to-six set was not made clear. At every age level, the researchers found, the social ages of the children were significantly higher than their mental and chronological ages. Their conclusion: Parents who push their children to be social may be causing neuroses in them.

"You have to look pretty sharp at what the parents have the children learn," says Professor John W. M. Whiting of Harvard's Laboratory of Human Development. *"What* they teach him is the clue to *why* they teach him. If they have the child running his legs off with lessons that carry a certain status value, such as French and tennis, it may be because they never had a chance to do these things themselves, and hope to attain the status through the achievements of the child." (The mechanism is viewed with endearing objectivity by one father who is rich, self-made, and the hardy survivor of a childhood sans French and tennis lessons: "My son associates with people of a higher level than I would have dared seek out. He gets to them through my success. He introduces me to their parents. You might say he pulls me up by my own bootstraps.

"His mother bought him a suit at Brooks Brothers and opened a charge account. He told me, 'Well, it's in your name, dad. You can use it too.' So he broke the ice for me. What did I know of such things? All I had was the money. He is my teacher, this kid, my social stepping-stone. He improves my standard of living.")

"All these parents want their children to be normal, well-adjusted people," says a psychologist at the Columbia University Bureau of Applied Social Research. "At the same time, they want them to be utterly unique, the most talented, intelligent, socially successful children in their group. So they push all the lessons and the social experience, which will make their children exceptional, and they note with satisfaction that all the other parents they know are doing it, too, which makes their children normal."

One need not, of course, restrict one's inquiries to academic circles to get knowledgeable opinion on the hows and whys of social precocity. One woman who runs an enormously successful modern dance school for children sees it all with admirable clarity. "There is tremendous pressure here for the children to learn social dancing," she says. "I don't teach it. I wouldn't if I were starving. [No matter, madam; others will.] Not all the children like to go to these classes, but the parents insist. These poor kids are dead, with all the activities they are pushed into . . . everything has to be done for them. Not, you find, because it's really for the children, but because the *mother* always wanted to sing or dance or whatever.

"It's a rat race. The parents start it and then the children get involved and it picks up momentum. One little girl, a pupil of mine, is a very talented dancer. This little girl goes to the basketball games on Saturday mornings with her fifth- and sixth-grade friends, and then they all go out to lunch together. She's got to be at the games because the boys are there, and so she skips the dancing lesson. I once told her mother this kind of activity was bad for her, that she was too young. The mother said it was good for children to become 'socially acclimated' at an early age. She said if her daughter learned now how to be at ease with boys and what to talk to them about, she would be more popular later on."

Group lessons in this school cost about $2.50 an hour, a very moderate price. The headmistress says that she doesn't like to give private lessons, which cost $15 an hour ("except for the very poor and the very talented"), and tries to dissuade the mothers who want them. But some parents insist—among them, says the lady, many who can't really afford it. "They have the idea that a private lesson makes it better, that they are doing more for the child. They do it because other parents do. If a woman's friends have their children learning the dance privately, she is ashamed to put her child into a group class."

The Westport mothers who nixed dancing for their sixth-graders are still in a distinct minority. It is not uncommon in many communities for the P.T.A. to sponsor social dancing classes, replete with white gloves, for its first- and second-graders. In one neighborhood the P.T.A. started its tots sharpening their footwork on the cha-cha at the age of five. One mother wanted nothing to do with it. But, she says, "My daughter came home one day and said, 'I want to go to dancing class.' I laughed and she started to cry. She said, '*Everybody* can do the cha-cha but me.' So I gritted my teeth and took her. I *hated* the idea, but there is no escape from all this stuff. It isn't really the dancing that matters, you understand. It is a sort of pre-sex training program."

(Apropos of which, several women in one group told their daughters of nine and ten not to let the boys "dance too close to them." "Why?" one youngster asked her parent. "I *like* to." The mother promptly withdrew her child from the class and went into extensive consultation with the school guidance counselor. "I think sex is their biggest worry," says a mother in this community. "It should be, too. If they are teaching children to dance at five and giving mixed parties for them at seven and warning them not to be sexy at ten, they damn well better *expect* trouble at fifteen.")

Dancing-school people being deeply aware of their responsibility to any budding wallflowers in the ranks, the course of instruction often includes far more than the dance per se. Much is made of "etiquette." One school emphasizes the principle of "social conscience," which a staff member elucidates thusly: "We teach that you have a social obligation toward any other human being. All your life you will run into people who will bore you. Nonetheless you must learn to deal with them and to make them comfortable. You have to learn certain rules, and the first rule is conversation."

Dedicated to this end, a social setting is simulated and the class proceeds as follows: Enter, shake hands when introduced

("Miss Fillmore," says the instructor, "may I present Master Whittaker?" "How do you do," says Miss Fillmore, age seven, languidly extending a white-gloved palm with a grace auguring the stuff of which debutantes are made), and look people straight in the eye. "All right," says the instructor. "Now, when I give the signal you will talk to the person on one side of you, and when I give another signal you will talk to the person on the other." He signals, and there is a polite buzz-z-z in one direction; he signals again, and there is a gentle hum-m-m in the other; dozens of tots, heads all cocked in nonchalant couplets, the conversation proceeding effortlessly, charmingly, in a devastating demonstration of burgeoning dinner-dance *savoir-faire.*

Dancing lends itself most readily to the competitive parental spirit, but other cultural pursuits can be similarly exploited. At the Wadsworth Atheneum in Hartford, Connecticut, which holds, as do many museums throughout the country, art classes (always oversubscribed) for children, a spokesman says:

"We take the children on a first come, first served basis. It has nothing to do with talent. But we find that the parent often is apt to feel his child is extra gifted. Some parents seem to want shortcuts to turn their children into clever performers. We have to tell them that this is not an art school for precocious children. We remind them that the purpose of art classes for children should be for the children's *own* pleasure. They all pay lip service to this idea, but I do not think it is their true motivation."

"In our exhibits," says the education program director of another museum, "we hang the work of all the children, and we try always to avoid indicating in any way which of them are more talented than others. For the children, raised in a highly competitive way, such a show of selectivity would be difficult, and for the parents it would be intolerable."

This man says most experts agree one can't be certain whether a child has true talent before he is eight or nine, but he has met many mothers who know better and have artistically gifted three-year-olds to prove it. Brooking no nonsense, a child psychologist says, "Phylogenetically, art ability is of much higher origin than, say, musical ability. You can be a very good musician and be of average intelligence, but art ability generally corelates with high intelligence. That is the reason we have musical prodigies, but no art prodigies—very small children do not have sufficiently developed intelligence." (That also may be the reason, he points out, that art lessons nowadays have significantly more prestige than music lessons.)

But musical ability is not to be knocked. Particularly in its more bravura forms, it can serve the competitive spirit right well. For example: "It is the absolute *end* to be able to say that your child is singing at the Met," says a New York mother who moves in opera-committee circles. Children's chorus auditions at the Metropolitan, she says, are attended by tots with their music and their voice coaches, and mothers who plead with the conductor to *understand:* that the child is over-wrought, burdened by laryngitis, exhausted from practice, and thus not in top form. "You find these kids who have been knocking themselves out on one lousy line from *Turandot.* One lousy line, in chorus, and it's not even sung onstage. And the mothers have had them working on it for weeks and weeks."

This informant reports further that there is a great striving among the mothers to make their young appear younger, since there isn't much call for children over ten. Thus auditions see large numbers of post-pubic girls with bosoms sternly compressed beneath their pink dresses, and large numbers of hairy chaps in sailor suits. One muscular boy, she recalls, stood upon the stage singing while his mother sat out front and kept time with a smil-ing nod. A suspicious soul sitting next to her asked how old the boy was. "Eight," said the mother, never losing a beat. "Tch, tch," said her neighbor, not at all *sotto voce.* "He must have a rare glandular disease."

The same notes echo, of course, in the grass-roots world of Clubs and Leagues. "I used to have a lot of trouble with parents whose children didn't get prizes at Pack meetings," says a former Cubmaster, dipping into the past with minimal nostalgia. "Once I was viciously attacked by a woman whose boy lost out in a kite-flying contest. We had words, and she hit me. Another time I had a bitter argument with an old friend because his son didn't get the Achievement Award for a model car. Of course they had built it together, and I guess the guy was disappointed, but he got so *nasty.* Finally I quit. The children were all right but the parents were impossible. I think kids, in a way, bring out the worst in people."

They are busy souls, these small gay blades—these prodigies and party givers. "And after all," says a child psychiatrist whose practice is, like the museum classes, always oversubscribed, "when you get the kind of child who is so busy that he can barely find an hour for *me*—then he generally has problems.

"The problems don't come because of all the child's activities, but because he has the kind of parents who find it necessary to push him so hard. Usually the parents who push socially are the same ones who push scholastically. They use their children the way they use their cars. The Old Rich, who have a secure social position, can treat their child like a banged-up station wagon. He can run around in blue jeans and torn sneakers and he doesn't have to win prizes for social or intellectual achievement. The lower classes, economically, are too busy getting along to use their children for anything except helping out, and so this kid, too, is a kind of station wagon—a practical conveyance. But the child of the ambitious middle class and the newly rich—ah, he is the Cadillac! He is an advance runner, you might say, for their own assault upon the social scale.

"It is the upper middle-class community that sets the fashion in these things, that first creates for its children a prematurely sophisticated milieu; and this fashion then filters down through the ranks, and we find those lower in the middle class—particularly professional people—re-creating this milieu as best they can."

An outstanding example of the above may be found in observation of Scarsdale, New York, which over the years has become one of the most maligned towns in the nation. Its good folk are bone-tired of being ribbed; and decency would compel one to leave them in peace did they not afford a microcosmic view of all that has been noted here. Scarsdale is, as now will be seen, archetypical of the child-centered community that produces the social child, and while it may suffer the jibes of the world at large, it should merit only thanks and hallelujahs from that chap who makes children's appointment books for a living.

IN THE COMMUNITY

A Great Place for Children

It is the considered, if largely unsubstantiated, theory of one forty-year resident of Scarsdale, New York, that her town owes much of its fame and most of its infamy to a gentleman named Hot Dog Joe.

Hot Dog Joe busied himself some years ago selling hot dogs near the Scarsdale High School. His trade was made somewhat difficult by a Village Board ordinance which forbade him to park his car near the school. The hot-dog-loving student body raised a mighty, albeit fruitless, protest in Joe's behalf, and their outcry traveled far, across the country, even across the waters and onto the pages of the Paris edition of the *New York Herald Tribune.*

The informant holds the view that Scarsdale never recovered from the hot-dog scandal. No town, she points out, can deprive kiddies of their hot dogs and expect the world to remember it kindly. It created the sort of situation out of which our most enduring public jokes are born, and the public has had a tendency to joke about Scarsdale ever since.

The probability is, however, that if Scarsdale children were indeed being deprived of hot dogs, it may be the only known occasion on which they have been deprived of anything at all, which renders dubious the connection between Hot Dog Joe and Scarsdale's renown. More likely, the place is famous because it is rich; because it is the suburban dream incarnate ("like a Deanna Durbin movie, all clean and unreal," Robert Paul Smith has said); because it breeds in fruitful numbers those Garden Club perennials—although they are largely slim and chic—upon whom Helen Hokinson based her immortal myth; and, finally, because it provides an almost painfully perfect model for child-directed communal life.

Scarsdale's child-centeredness is, of course, not typical of child-centeredness in general, any more than Scarsdale itself is typical of communities in general. It is, rather, a pace-setter; from here all moves downward, to be copied as faithfully as the budget will permit. Or, as a family welfare worker in neighboring White Plains says, "Let's say Scarsdale and other towns like it are the couturier originals. A year or two later you'll find $12.95 copies all over the country, and darn good copies, too."

Scarsdale itself, lying in the loamy oasis of Westchester County some twenty miles from New York City, is a village and/or town of some eighteen thousand residents. It houses impressive numbers of lawyers, brokers, professors, and assorted shoguns of commerce, almost all of whom commute to New York. There is no industry in the village—or, as the citizenry likes to say, "Scarsdale's only industry is its schools." It would be more accurate, probably, to say that Scarsdale's only industry is its children.

Indeed, but for children there might be no Scarsdale. The acknowledged motive of most people who move here from elsewhere is to bring their young into this eminently desirable fold: a superb school system, a staggering roster of community activities, and a perfectly splendid assortment of Joneses, j.g., to keep up with.

"The tendency is for people not to move here until they have children of school age," says an executive in the school system. When asked why they like Scarsdale, residents almost unfailingly speak as parents—"It's a great place to bring up children"—and many, who find the town overorganized, over-refined, overprivileged, and middling dull, say they wouldn't have come in the first place "if it weren't for the kids."

The average income in Scarsdale is estimated at just a shade under $30,000, and the town looks it. It is a singularly pretty place, with a heavy leaning toward English Tudor and street after street of downright baronial homes, many costing upwards of $100,000. There is a local story, which has been circulated widely, concerning a class of first-graders who were assigned to write essays about their families. One child wrote: "Once there was a family that was very poor. The father was poor. The mother was poor. The little girl was poor. The chauffeur was poor. . . ." The story is not at all unlikely. It is perfectly possible for a child to live past high-school age in Scarsdale without seeing anyone at work except the help at home and the few traders in the village square.

This fact has inspired much criticism of the good Scarsdale life, from within as well as without, although few residents ever get sufficiently perturbed to pack up and move. Teachers in the school system, most of whom live elsewhere ("We can't afford it"), express the opinion that Scarsdale's rarefied homogeneity creates an unwholesome atmosphere for children.

"Kids grow up thinking the rest of the world lives just as they do," one says. "I wouldn't live here even if I could. I wouldn't want my boys growing up in all this. Too many people in this town make great financial sacrifices to move to Scarsdale, and they push their kids into everything to associate them with the 'right' children. There are simply too many pressures on the kids."

One longtime resident, a former newspaperwoman who stayed on after her children were grown to become a ranking Critic From Within, says: "I've lived here forty years and seen it change from a pleasant country town to this damnably child-dominated place. And none of it is unique to Scarsdale, either. It's a national disease, all this child nonsense, but more money is poured into it here.

"A community like Scarsdale gives children an extended sense of their importance. I heard a woman, a Scarsdale woman, call the Board of Education to say that her child had been rude to her and what should she do? Can you imagine! A lot of parents around here are scared to death of their kids. When I brought up four daughters I didn't give a hoot in hell whether they liked me or not. They learned to respect me and all adults, and now they're nice, healthy adults themselves.

"I can remember a doctor, a pediatrician, who left here a while back to go to Baltimore. I said, 'Why are you leaving us?' He said, 'Tell me, what is your theory of child-raising?' I said, 'Carefully supervised neglect.' And he said, 'Well, if more of the mothers around here felt the way you do I wouldn't be leaving.' God knows what he found in Baltimore."

Carefully supervised neglect is, most assuredly, not the prevalent mode in Scarsdale. So busy are the waking hours of its children that a teacher in one of the elementary schools was moved, not so long ago, to take a class poll of what her charges did with their free time. She found that, generally speaking, they had none. Here are some of the good works that kept them busy:

For the sake of its children, Scarsdale maintains a true-blue scouting spirit. Little boys are almost automatically Cub Scouts and little girls almost invariably Brownies and most of them generally go on to scouthood proper, spurred by the energies of participating parents.

There are six neighborhood associations, and in each a militant P-T Association which supplies a welter of activities for the children in conjunction with their school programs, most notably the aforementioned P-T sponsored dance lessons. Some of the elementary schools also provide cooperative dance programs in after-school hours and *in addition to* those under P-T sponsorship.

There is a flourishing Community Workshop which has classes all year in just about anything "cultural, educational, or recreational."

There is some form of after-school religious instruction for most Scarsdale children; also, a heavy schedule of church social programming for the young.

There are cooperative nurseries, where mothers volunteer one afternoon a week; and then, of course, there are the private nurseries, well attended.

There are dizzying numbers of after-school clubs—the high school alone has fifty such. There is a children's section of the Bridge Club. There is a children's section of the Garden Club, and garden shows for the young. There are myriad special events, such as live dramatic performances, puppet shows, touring art shows with fine works borrowed from museums. ("I daresay reproductions wouldn't be classy enough for Scarsdale children," says one wag.) Across the town line, in Larchmont, the story is told that when the Women's Book

Club organized a Book Fair for children and called upon the public to donate, it received some two hundred first editions of children's classics from Scarsdale residents alone. "It could only happen in Scarsdale," says a Larchmonter, only a trifle resentfully.

There is the gamut—wider, perhaps, here than in other communities—of private lessons in which parents enroll their young. Music and dancing are very big. So is private instruction in art and languages, generally French.

There is a Village Recreation Department, handsomely housed, heavily staffed, and with a truly stupendous roster of activities. It operates year-round, but winter is a somewhat heavier season since in summer a large number of Scarsdale children go to camp or abroad.

There is, finally, an outstanding public school system, from which all else radiates outward. It has been created and is maintained under the close, unblinking eye of a citizenry that holds education dear, and Ivy League education sacred.

A Board of Education man estimates that 85 to 87 per cent of Scarsdale children go on to four-year college; 94 to 97 per cent end up with some form of higher education. Thus Scarsdale schools are almost exclusively college-preparatory. "If a student has vocational needs," says the Board man, "we bring somebody in to fill them or we pay for him to get them elsewhere."

In Scarsdale parents keep a heavy hand on the educational rudder. The P-T associations frequently hold workshops to do special studies in teaching techniques, and make their reports to the executive boards of the schools. Many parent groups have paid consultants to tell them, as one observer says, "What to do with a five-year-old in education—that sort of thing." All parent groups except that of the high school have fund-raising events each year. The high school has a parent-sponsored scholarship fund. One elementary school has a Science Park, budgeted by the parents; any requests made of the parents for extra material or equipment is generally and cheerfully granted.

The Town Club, a potent village force of some one thousand male residents, once appointed a committee to look into Scarsdale education. Hiring a Columbia University professor full time ("to get the *facts,*" one man said ominously, although, heaven knows, there are few facts that the school system is able to keep from parents), they found that collegians who had been "A" students in the high school were making a "C," or average, showing at Harvard. The gentlemen were greatly agitated, and pressured the school administration to look once again into its own techniques—because, they reasoned, if *Scarsdale* stock was doing less than splendidly at Cambridge, something must be wrong with the local school system.

Such parental determination to get into the act—typical of the Scarsdale stance on anything concerning its children—has, naturally enough, kicked up traces of resentment on the school staffs from time to time. While a highly placed school official states for publication, "There is absolutely no friction between the parents and teachers," he concedes in private that, "These parent groups can be a pain in the neck. They're all experts. I sometimes don't think the average parents here really care whether or not their child is getting the best kind of education *for him,* as long as he's getting the kind that will get him into the right college."

To this end, what is virtually a private school system has been carved out of the public schools. There are seven schools —five elementary, one junior high, one high school—staffed by 287 professional people, including 247 classroom teachers and 4 full-time psychologists. The typical teacher who comes into the Scarsdale school system has a master's degree and five years' experience. The salary schedule is very high: the median salary for teachers is about $9,700 with a ceiling for Ph.D's of $12,000. In the past, citizens' committees have met with the educators to review the salary system and decide whether to hand out still more money or longer sabbaticals.

"This town demands the best for its children," says a Scarsdalian, "and nobody worries how much it will cost. These kids are hell-bent for Harvard and Vassar, and the parents are making sure they have every damn thing they need to get there."

To enhance the private school aura, two of the elementary schools have libraries with huge, open fireplaces, before which, of a nippy winter's day, a teacher can seat tots upon the floor and by flickering light read to them soft and low. "Can you imagine the associations later in life?" says a lady from White Plains, where there is nary a fireplace in the school libraries. "Those children will *love to read!*"

The high school, a solid structure impressively wrought in bastard Tudor, has voluminous parking space filled, in season, not merely with cars but with Thunderbirds (a favored sixteenth-birthday present), Corvettes, and the like. (The space can be handily adapted to other purposes, as well. "It gets flooded out there in heavy rains," says a teacher, "and one day after school I looked out the window and saw two boys fooling around with sailboats—and they *weren't toys.*") Much can be told about the ownership of any car on high-school grounds at a glance: if it is a low-cost model and more than three years old, chances are it belongs to a teacher.

A couple of years back, the teachers complained that they couldn't find any parking space. The administration decided that one must at some point stand firm against the young— brave words in Scarsdale—and made bold to restrict parking space to seniors and such juniors as lived beyond walking distance to the school (a difficult distance to measure in this day). The restriction, of course, was short-lived, and the final solution pure Scarsdale: they built a second parking lot.

Not to be outdone by their high-school siblings, many of Scarsdale's younger citizens also move about on wheels. Electrified miniature sports cars, costing upwards of $450 and commonly known as toys, have been popular in the community since they were first put on the market. "I was in a neighbor's home," a Scarsdalian reported not long ago, "when his ten-year-old boy came running into the house and said, 'Hey, dad, can I have one of those electric cars?' His father said, 'Are you nuts? You expect me to spend $500 for a toy for you?' The kid said, 'Aw, dad, *everybody* has one!' And this fellow went out and looked around the block and, sure enough, everybody did."

"In a very real sense," says a psychologist, "children out here run their families and set the pace of community life. After all, there is nothing else *in* Scarsdale, just houses with people living in them and taking care of their children. There is little more to do or worry about, so they spend inordinate amounts of time doing *that*.

"The mother keeps her children busy partly to give herself free time. But this doesn't mean she is any the less child-centered. She takes that free time and goes off to a lecture on child guidance, or has lunch with her girl friends and talks about children. This is what we really mean by the child-centered community: not that the parents are always *with* the children, but that so many of their energies are involved in planning *around* the children."

By way of illustration he points out the workings of the Village Recreation Department, which is, as one might expect in a community focused on children, a Very Important institution. It is a venture of corporate proportions employing, in one way or another, the active services, financial aid, or at very least the moral support and guidance of most of the child-bearing adults in town.

Among the entertainments shepherded by the department: baseball leagues (Scarsdale has no Little League) with a total of 84 teams; basketball leagues (165 teams); football, soccer, and softball leagues (38 teams in the girls' pre-high-school set alone); lacrosse, dog obedience courses, table-tennis tourneys, photography contests, talent shows, indoor and outdoor movies; a wide range of non-league athletic activities carried out, on Saturdays, in fourteen gymnasiums in seven schools, and all sorts of special holiday programs.

Christmas shows for children, given in school auditoriums, are produced under the auspices of the Recreation Department and sponsored by such as the Scarsdale Elks Club. (During this season, children may drop their letters to Santa into special mailboxes installed courtesy of the Scarsdale Chamber of Commerce and get replies on his personal stationery, courtesy of the junior division of the Scarsdale Women's Club.)

The Recreation Department also provides coordination and equipment for July Fourth programs conducted by the various neighborhood associations and, in the Hallowe'en season, lends spiritual guidance to an Annual Window Painting Contest sponsored by the Chamber of Commerce. To this purpose local merchants lend their windows, and results are judged by a team of experts supplied through the cooperation of the Scarsdale Art Association. ("I would say," comments a local educator, "that the recreation program is unwholesomely competitive." "We are often accused," says the recreation director, "of being too competitive. But I would say that the business of education in this town is much more so.")

In summer, however, the Recreation Department really serves with bells on. Where most communities have playgrounds, Scarsdale has play schools (for children four to eight) and day camps (nine to fifteen), embodying the usual stress on arts and crafts, music, dance, woodworking, and athletics, and attended by one teacher for every twenty children. For these, as for most of its programs, the Recreation Department has available all the facilities of all the schools in town. There are also picnics, field trips, shows and concerts, children's theater, playground olympics, and (a big factor in Scarsdale: these young may one day play on top campus courts) tennis clinics.

The trouble is that although there is this staggering assortment of things for Scarsdale children to do, not many stick around to do them. Those who are not at vacation resorts with their parents are away at camp (it is estimated that more than 50 per cent of the village young go to private camp) or involved in other private, organized activities.

So depleted, in fact, are the ranks of Scarsdale's young in summer that even the ice-cream wagon entrepreneurs have a difficult time surviving. A case in point is Mel the Good Humor Man, who sells his wares in next-door Larchmont but puts thumbs down on Scarsdale, "because it is a lousy territory. The kids all disappear as soon as school is out." (In Larchmont, however, Mel does right well. He is a man of proven stature in the community: after eleven years the Good Humor people changed his route, whereupon the children of Larchmont signed fifteen hundred names upon a petition to bring him back, and back he came.)

Among stories of lonely summers, a tearjerker is reported by one Scarsdale woman whose daughter was kept home from camp last year because of low-grade anemia. The child was moping around the house one tepid August day, distracting her parent greatly. "Can't you find something to do?" said the mother. "Go play with your friends." "I *can't* play with my friends," came the reply. "They're all in Europe."

Thus it may be seen that Organization is essential to the leisure hours of a Scarsdale child, and the adults strive tirelessly, and at considerable personal sacrifice, to provide it. One cannot truly appreciate the extent to which Scarsdale parents are involved in the recreational life of their young unless one understands the philosophy of the Dads' Clubs, a cornerstone of local culture.

The Dads' Clubs are groups of Scarsdale fathers organized to help their children take athletic recreation, apparently on the premise that no Pop who's a real Pop lets his offspring play alone. They help primarily by coaching, for which purpose the Recreation Department offers a Coaching for Dads course, and by footing the bills, which they know how to do blindfolded.

"We have seven Dads' Clubs in the village," says the town's Recreation Director, "with two to three hundred men in each. The dads of all elementary school children are asked to join when their children reach certain grades—fourth grade for boys, fifth for girls. The Recreation Department brings all the pupils of the same grade together in athletic events. The dads coach the games and supply the uniforms and other equipment. For baseball, for example, we supply the balls; they supply everything else.

"All the clubs are incorporated. For each sport, there is a Central Dads' Committee to which each Dads' Club sends a representative. They set up rules for each game.

"I suppose Dads' Clubs are a bone of contention among the educators," he concedes, "but we think they are fine."

His optimism is not shared by all Dads' Club dads. "It is a damn nuisance, let me tell you," says one. "I coach baseball.

Some of these youngsters are impossible to work with. They have never been told 'no.' I once told one of the boys on my team, 'If you don't do it as I tell you, don't come back,' and he almost went into shock.

"And a lot of them don't even *want* to play. That burns me up. Many's the Saturday morning three or four kids have shown up on the field and I've had to get on the phone and try to round up a team, pleading with the others to come play ball.

"Good God, when I was a kid we would have died of embarrassment if our fathers had come to watch us play. We never got much chance to play, anyway—the bigger kids were always chasing us off the field. Nowadays we not only coach for them, we protect the field for them so every boy will have his chance—and we have to beg them to show up." (One recalls the courageous stance taken by Walter Kerr, *New York Herald Tribune* drama critic and a Westchester resident, who has expressed the opinion that if there is one place his boys *don't* need him, it is on the ball field.)

Another Scarsdale dad tells a pitiful tale of Saturday mornings spent delivering boys to the playing field "when I could have been on that beautiful green. I could cry just thinking of it." He had twelve boys on his team and was obliged to make two trips, to the far reaches of Scarsdale and back, to collect them all. It was, our man says, a terrible lot of driving. One Saturday morning he rebelled. He made an impassioned plea to the boys to tell their parents to drive them to the field. The next Saturday came, and no parents showed up—but three chauffeurs did.

"It works out quite well," says the Recreation man. "All our youth programs do. After all, we have some of the best organizational brains in the country helping us out."

Some of the best organizational brains in the country may, in fact, be found in the ranks of the Dads' Clubs themselves. Here are kings of commerce coaching basketball, panjandrums of the law arguing an out at third base. Of all the proud memories of years past, one resident's favorite is of a game at which the president of the Carnegie Foundation and the president of the Rockefeller Foundation were out on the football field holding the tape (this was, of course, before Dean Rusk left the community for points south).

"We fill a real need, and most of our fathers are fine sports about it," says one dedicated Dads' Club man, pondering the point long and cautiously. "But I would not say that this town has given its heart and soul to the children. There is no bowling, no outdoor skating rink, no community hall exclusively for the youngsters."

That's what the man said. And these words of stinging criticism may be just what a Scarsdale lady, one of the founders of the Community Workshops of Scarsdale and a herculean worker in that cause, means when she says:

"The children's lives here are not overorganized. They are underorganized. A group of mothers started the Community Workshops originally feeling that there was a need here that was not being fulfilled." What with the schools, P.T.A.'s, Recreation Department, community classes, cooperative nurseries, Dads' Clubs, den mothers, and Dance Centers at work, it is difficult to imagine what that need was. However, to continue:

"We are a nonprofit institution to supplement existing facilities in the community. Parents and children can get instruction here in just about anything they want. Say a woman calls up and asks for guitar lessons for her child. If we can get enough others interested to make the group financially self-sustaining, we start a guitar course. We teach in homes or in rented space. We get teachers from universities or wherever.

"It is a great deal of work, but most gratifying. When we started Community Workshops, the mothers who organized it put in at least three mornings a week and worked during the wee hours of the night. They began to forget what their families looked like. We are rolling along splendidly now, but we still work hard. We have dance groups and, in the languages, everything from French and Spanish to Russian and Japanese.

"We also run our own cooperative nurseries, but we try to avoid ending up as a baby-sitting service by insisting that the parents chaperone the children and help with the work. At the same time, of course, we are giving the parent an opportunity to work in a group where she can observe a child with his peers, and where she can relate to her own children, too. [*There* we go.] We also have a group of child study courses that are particularly popular with the mothers. We have had Early School Years, Methods of Speech Therapy, Local Mores, and Human Relations."

There are, in Scarsdale and environs, about two dozen pediatricians ("all doing marvelously well," says an insider); ten diaper services; at least three baby-sitting services; twenty-five toy stores ("Whatever these kids want, they get; don't worry"), and some fifteen local psychiatrists. The latter are, perhaps, busiest of all. One says:

"The headaches of seeing that your boy keeps up his marks so he can get into Princeton, of hanging on to social status and trying to gain more of it *through him*—all this is bound to cause some pressures and tensions in the family. People here expect to live vicariously, through their children—they are unable to accept the child for himself."

Another: "My wife and I seldom accept dinner invitations here. The place is so appallingly wrapped up in children. You go over to somebody's house and the kiddies are brought on to serve canapés, and then you spend the rest of the evening talking about children and the problems of being a parent. For a psychiatrist, of course, it's impossible. They get me cornered and don't let up. I am becoming dangerously hostile."

A third: "The parents here are slaves to their children. They are constantly involved, car-pooling them or supervising them or planning for them or talking about them. Children, children, children. This is a middle-class disease, and, of course, in an upper-middle-class community like Scarsdale, it grows even worse.

"They have such deep feelings of inadequacy as parents that they try to feel better about themselves by pushing the children into things. This gives them a sense of freedom and at the same time makes them feel that they are doing more for the children.

"Actually, what they are doing for the children is making them completely dependent. If you took one of these kids away from organized activity and put him out to fend for himself, he would be lost. Utterly lost."

And, finally, there is the voice of the child, belonging in this case—although it could belong to a good many children in Scarsdale—to a junior-high-schooler, age twelve: "Ohh-h," it wails. "Oh, what a town! You could just *die of boredom.*"

IN STYLE
How to Wear a Child

TRIOLET ON A FLAT FAILURE

Poor child, she's ten years old today,
And has no bosoms yet.
No wonder life looms flat and gray.
Poor child, she's ten years old today,
Much too depressed to run and play.
Her shame, she can't forget.
Poor child, she's ten years old today,
And has no bosoms yet.

This lament for our times appeared a while back in *Women's Wear Daily,* generally acknowledged bible of the garment industry. It was authored by a lady executive in the trade, in heartfelt protest against the retail debut of a contrivance known as the "training bra," a shapeless wisp of lace available in size 28AA, which evokes a near-concave image and provides mainly spiritual support for moppets who have, as yet, no need for pectoral containment.

Despairing sonnets may yet be written about the frightening precocity of the young, the mournful loss of innocence; to no avail. What to some may seem a symbol of perdition is to the child a symbol of status and, to the child worshiper, a symbol of all those worthy works that expedite the development of social skills. The 28AA is doing smashingly well. Fashion people say it is a favored birthday gift for ten-, nine-, and even eight-year-olds.

"Girls are growing older, *younger* all the time!" rhapsodized an advertisement appearing not long ago in behalf of a teen-agers' magazine. "They want their first nylons younger . . . They wear their first black dress younger . . . They wheedle their first 'high' heels younger . . . They buy their first lipstick younger . . . They put on their first girdle younger . . . They experience their first bras younger . . . They date younger . . . They 'steady' younger. It's the tempo-allegro of the times. Everything happens faster, quicker, sooner, younger . . . even adolescence. Girls are teen before their time—at tenteen, eleventeen and twelveteen."

Indeed, indeed. In this intoxicating tempo-allegro climate, suburban beauty shops across the country cater to ten-year-olds who know what they want, and it isn't a Dutch Bob. The tots hold standing Saturday appointments and emerge with their coiffures ("more hair than face," one salon owner observes) lacquered against the breezes. In department stores and baby boutiques, trade is forever brisk in party wear for social two-year-olds; bikinis (in season) sell like rattles for the preschool resort crowd, and velvet at-home pants are a big item for those who must stay in town. Famous French couturiers are creating high-style originals, with paralyzing price tags, for the three- to six-year-old set, which home-grown designers promptly copy, or knock off, at budget and not-so-budget prices—all beamed at the mother who would make claim to the chicest child in town.

At birthday parties attended by Junior Leaguers-in-training, four-year-olds wear custom-made pinafores with the nonchalance of a society matron sporting a little black nothing of a $300 dress. Even at less swank gatherings the toddler wears a dress that is, if not custom-made, Made in France or at least Made in Italy. Her gloves are as impeccably white as those of the upper classes, her underpinnings just as lacy and her manner, mildly disquieting in one so young, that of a child who knows it's a free country and she, too, can grow up to make the Ten Best-Dressed list if she puts her shoulder to the wheel.

In short, not all the preschool mannequins on view these days are necessarily daughters of rich parents, although it helps. But they all *are* daughters of women dedicated to the principle that it is never too soon to start teaching a girl that some of the best things in life are wearable.

This is the kind of principle dear to the heart of the children's wear industry. "I sometimes think," a manufacturer of baby clothes mused recently, "that what's wrong with kids, psychologically, is that parents put them into any old thing. The child who doesn't see a smart-looking little lady when she looks in the mirror never gets a chance to develop what you might call a sense of emotional security. Then she grows up and what have you got? A neurotic, that's what."

Thus assured of their social responsibility, the children's wear people work hard to fulfill it, and by and large do a fine job. The above-mentioned chap, for example, a high-price leader in the field, sends his designers to Europe every year ("Twelve countries, I send them to"), just as his colleagues in the women's wear industry do, to note what the best children are wearing. Culling his line, a mother may insure her child's emotional security with a dress that retails for $150 (this, of course, is for the copy; the Paris original costs $225). Admittedly, such gowns are only for important occasions. This manufacturer estimates that, in truly well-dressed circles, the everyday frock worn by a three- to six-year-old—that is, the dress in which she will go to nursery school or knock about the house—averages about $35. Since it is estimated that a growing girl's clothes have a life expectancy of a year and a half, the cost could be amortized at slightly less than $2 a month, which, come to think of it, may be a bargain.

The three-year-old who is dressing in this price range obviously required a solid start and may be one of the lucky tykes who wore a christening dress costing $1,100. They are sold (mail orders accepted) by an ultra-plush New York concern, perhaps on the theory that the sooner one learns the feel of good fabric the harder it will be to forget. While these are a limited item, many stores report selling christening dresses "in volume" at $100. Mink-collared coats are popular for babies, though not for infants under one, because, as one buyer from Saks Fifth Avenue explains, they spit, and this can be had for fur.

Such mundanities do not deter a furrier, Georges Kaplan—who gives little girls mink stoles for their dolls whenever he sells mama a mama-size stole—from making fur-lined carriage robes for infants. He calls them "brainwashing in the cradle" and offers them in two models: chinchilla-lined for rich rich babies and Persian-lamb-lined for poor rich babies. Further, he does a thriving business making little girls' mink coats, at $1,800 apiece, although this can prove a hazardous race against time: the three-year-old may have outgrown her mink before her monogram has been sewn into the lining.

Expensive fur coats for children are thought to be in

questionable taste, however, by the mother who has a Gift for Fashion. She knows strict rules govern the attire of children who would be chic, and the first of these is to avoid over-statement. Hand embroidery, for example, is fine, but too-obvious hand embroidery is pretentious. The best kind is white on white, which speaks volumes of the right sort, but quietly. In the trade, the white-on-white number is known as the "grandmother dress"—i.e., the expensive, wildly impractical sort of item that grandmothers love to buy.

The second rule is that little girls should look like little girls. It is utterly bad form to make them look like midgets. The fashionable look for, say, a three-year-old changes from time to time, just as it does for her mother (a mode of recent seasons is described by one designer as "a little bit of Victorian coupled with a soupçon of exotic French, with some Casual California thrown in"), but it is always uniquely suited to three-year-olds.

Beyond these basic requirements are countless lesser rules, and the mother who wants to start her child off right had best heed them carefully. One mother, exceedingly knowledgeable in such matters, suggests a partial list of pointers for dressing girls under six:

GOOD: Smocking on dresses; brown or red shoes for in-formal wear; black patent leather shoes for parties ("Patent shoes on the street, with a tailored dress," she notes, "would be a dead giveaway; that mother just doesn't *know*"); simple sailor hats; French or Swiss labels for dresses, British labels for coats; hand-knit wool blankets for carriages.

BAD: Excessive use of pink ("Black is smart for parties"); overly long dresses ("Dresses for little girls should always look a wee bit small"); waistlines ("They don't have waists and you shouldn't pretend they do; their dresses should hang loose from the shoulders"); flowered bonnets of the Bo-Peep variety;

carriage covers that say "My name is ————"; snowsuits ("Passé. The proper outfit is a pair of leggings, well-tailored, with a neat, strict little tweed coat").

The anti-snowsuit edict applies as firmly to little boys, for whom, it develops, a similarly helpful list of do's and don'ts can be compiled. Thus, short pants and knee socks—solid color, though a discreet cable stitch is permitted—are warmly endorsed for preschool boys. Cardigan jackets and Eton caps are excellent, as are white or striped shirts, open at the neck. Velvet pants are good for parties—"but short. The long ones are a bit pretentious."

Cowboy shirts, black shoes, and argyle socks should be avoided. Neckties constitute a gross gap in taste, as do tweedy sports jackets tailored on adult lines, long-trousered suits, and fedora hats—anything, in short, that makes a boy look like a miniature man.

Blue jeans for either sex, be it noted, are acceptable around horses, boats, and back yards, but not for street wear. Further, parents are urged to restrict their daughter's pants-wearing. ("Little girls who run around in pants all the time never learn to sit or walk properly. Pants have become popular because nobody has laundresses any more, but this is the kind of hardship one must rise above.")

Carriages, too, are tremendously important in the fashion picture, inasmuch as they furnish one of the earliest opportunities to establish one's status in public. The smartest models are British, high-wheeled, leather-lined and easy on the chrome. Navy blue, for example, with white or gray lining, is considered a felicitous choice. In circles where most families employ nurses or other baby-tenders, low wheels or low handlebars—anything that requires the help to lean over—constitutes a very bad *gaffe*, almost as inexcusable as having no help at all. On the other hand, the unfortunate woman who wheels her own should not try to overcompensate with rolling finery ("rather like wearing sable on a bus"). For *her*, a baby carriage is optimally plaid canvas ("the Ivy League look; it's not really upper class, it's simply the American idea of upper class, but it will do"), low in the wheels, honestly and unashamedly itself. (Down on this level, incidentally, crew cuts are favored for boys, as is an emphasis on gray flannel and denim—"inexpensive and inoffensive"—when dressing older children.)

As to the accouterments of carriage travel, they are, in high-wheel society, ideally white on white, and nifty sets composed of single sheet and single cover may be had in tasteful lace and ribbon at prices ranging from $350 downward, although several buyers agree that the average price for everyday strolling linen is $25 the set; *but these are* verboten *on any carriage without a nurse at the helm*. Very acceptable mohair blankets of Scottish descent, costing about $10, may be used with propriety in the plaid canvas carriage.

Thus it is not essential to pay a great deal to outfit the chic tyke. As one designer points out, Good Taste will triumph over any financial handicap. True, she says, "it's hard to find simple, smart things in moderate-priced children's clothes. The Europeans do that sort of thing *so* well, but simplicity is expensive in this country. Most of our manufacturers make cute little pokey party dresses, pink and ruffles—dreadful. But fortunately, the situation is improving. People are becoming more conscious of the fact that children should be fashionably dressed. Some designers are creating the Simple Little Nothing at a really low price, particularly in sports clothes, and the customer who dresses smartly herself will buy it for her child."

As evidence, the lady points to the fact that the Simple Little Nothings she sells through chi-chi stores at chi-chi prices do just as well in certain large chain emporia for the masses where her designs are merchandised under another label. "Good muddy colors, dark, funny little prints—they are the biggest sellers in my lower-priced lines. I tell you, American taste is rising rapidly in all price ranges. I am very optimistic. Very optimistic."

Acknowledged a potent factor in this heartening ascension of taste is Caroline Kennedy, an incalculable influence on little girls' clothing styles for the past several years. In the first months of Mr. Kennedy's administration, when the heart of the nation's garment industry lay in throbbing anticipation on the front stoop of the White House, many designers broke their backs trying to get advance word on what Caroline was going to wear. Mrs. Kennedy, to her immortal credit, provided little cooperation, and one stylist had her knuckles rapped for leaking drawings of several Caroline purchases to the garment trade press. It soon became apparent, at any rate, that Caroline's fashion philosophy hewed closely to her mother's, and the industry sped into production on the easy, sporting Little Nothing Look (also known as the Least Look, the Spare Look, the Clean Look, the Bare Look) that had been and still is endorsed from the top.

More recently the White House has done its bit for little boys. John Kennedy, Jr., appeared on front pages across the country last Easter, sporting the bangs-in-the-eyes coif worn by Prince Charles in his knee-britches days and still favored by European royalty. This engendered some criticism from anti-royalty types (in a newspaper poll of public opinion on John, Jr.'s hairdo, one reader uncharitably declared: "He looks like they can't afford to get his hair cut"), but it also inspired a trend. Barbers in three cities, questioned two weeks after John, Jr., got his picture in the papers, reported significant numbers of mothers leading in their crew-cut young and asking the man to "Shape it, please, so I can let it grow out like this"

—proffering up John's photograph. Subsequently, perhaps bowing to the heavy weight of majority opinion, John got his hair cut; what his tonsorial disciples did is unknown.

Though his own britches and bangs are, alas, gone with the years, the image of a younger Prince Charles lingers on persistently, albeit with modifications, as the image of chic boyhood personified. "We still like that spiffy Charlie look," says one authority who manufactures a high-status line of little-boy clothes. "That haircut is still very smart, very good. But the total effect has changed a bit. Nowadays we like a boy to look British in a Frenchy sort of way. We make a pant length somewhere between the very short French pant and the longer British. We love the Eton jacket suit, but we do it in more decorative colors and materials, a bit more Gallic. But the basic elements of tailoring remain British all the way; they are the best, of course. We shape the pant to flatter a fat or a scrawny leg. We use a high-rise waist to soften that tummy. We take the child's figure, which is short and squat and has a backside and many other inelegances, and we camouflage it. The clothes are witty. Today a mother can have the same pleasure dressing boys as girls. Our little fellows look neat, trim, and sophisticated."

"They look like jerks," a department store executive says privately. "If mothers could, they'd keep the poor kids in those Prince Charlie get-ups until high school. I just hate to think what the consequences might be."

This is a minority view. Most high-style advocates for children are apt to explain that fashion is *good* for them. "If you dress a child well and make him conscious of his clothes, he will form good habits and look like a gentleman," says a children's wear buyer. "If you let him run around in blue jeans all the time he will grow up looking like a bum and his wife will have a devil of a time getting him to change his socks or put on a tie." Further, children enjoy fashion: "They are very vain. They love to look at themselves in the mirror. You watch a little girl, even at five, trying on a dress, and wherever there is any indication of a future figure she will say, 'Pull it tight.' They take an interest in shopping, and sometimes their taste is better than their parents'. We had one four-year-old come in here, head right for the rack, and pick out a dress that was just perfect for her. The mother had her heart set on another dress, and this child said, 'Oh, mother, don't buy that, I'll *never* wear it.' And you know, she was perfectly right. The dress just wasn't *her* at all."

Traditionally, mothers like shopping for five-year-olds, who are pliable, and suffer untold spiritual damage shopping for thirteen-year-olds, who stand militantly on the threshold of their own fashion convictions. Today this distinction is archaic, there being hardly a five-year-old around anymore who, buoyed up by lessons in self-expression and early social development, doesn't have convictions. The point is lamentably well documented by a study done by the New York State College of Home Economics, which probed the psychology of shopping habits of five- to nine-year-old girls. It was found that they had "an amazing amount of independent taste" and exercised it fully. All the mothers interviewed admitted they were fearful of risking a scene in front of salesladies and invariably gave in to their daughters' whims. This abject parental capitulation was hailed in the women's pages, which know their customers, under such headlines as: "A Woman Is Never Too Young to Fight for Her Fashion Rights." Said one editorial believer fervently: "The wise mother will not stifle her daughter's fashion instincts. The child is learning how to be a *woman*."

A little girl set upon enhancing her native fashion sense will find a host of fashion authorities eager to teach her how to pick her best colors, how to walk, how to style her hair. Certain large and well-known department stores, for example, have long run what are known as charm or beauty schools, wherein the neophyte teen-ager might get a grasp on the fundamentals of womanhood. But neophyte teen-agers are rare nowadays, and the doors have been thrown open to those hordes of pre-teens who are, as the adman says, growing older, *younger*, all the time, and thus can no longer be denied. One such commercial dispenser of charm and beauty enrolls in the junior division of its popular academy of charm twelve-, eleven-, and ten-year-olds—and has just barely been able to hold the line against the urgent pleas of nine-year-olds and their mothers. It is a four-week, five-dollar course, conducted in an ivy-shorn hall filled with four to five hundred gloriously attentive youngsters, and the curriculum is a corker.

The first week is given over to grooming and hair care. The girls are taught how to apply cold cream—but not makeup, says a spokesman sternly, "because we don't feel they're really quite ready." A gentleman from the store's adult beauty salon serves as consultant, advising each child, after exhaustive consideration, what hair style does the most for her, and teaching her to set and comb it. "We discourage hair teasing and sophisticated styles," a lady from the academy of charm says, "but many of the girls want them, even though it's really not chic anymore. If a girl is really determined to have a big *bouffant* 'do', we try at least to tone it down. I must say, the way some of the older [i.e., eleven- and twelve-year-old] girls come in here, with their hair teased six inches high and their faces covered with makeup, just about anything we do would be an improvement. We do try to give them looks that are smart, but appropriate to their age."

The second week is devoted to fashion coordination. In this phase the assembled trainees, appetites whetted and

thirsting now for greater knowledge, absorb invaluable pointers on how to put together an outfit with flair and éclat, how
to develop a personal style, and how to stretch one's wardrobe
by an imaginative interplay of accessories.

In the third week the tender novitiate is instructed in what
is called the "fashion-model walk"—head high, shoulders
back, chest thrust proudly out to make those little training
bras sing sweet songs of future splendor, tummy tucked in
firmly ("That *does* give us trouble," says our lady ruefully.
"You can't do much about the tummy if there is no waist"),
hips moving smoothly, rhythmically—but not too ostenta-
tiously—above legs shod often as not in nylon and perched on
slim-heeled shoes ("I tell them we don't really approve of
heels for girls under thirteen, and they all fall on the floor
laughing"). This is not, of course, the officially endorsed
fashion-model walk—chest concave, chin menacingly down,
shoulders and pelvis thrust forward—but it is considered a
more appropriate stance for ten-year-olds and will with time
and luck surely evolve into something better.

The fourth and last week of the course is marked by a
"fashion-show graduation," wherein each tyke takes to the
runway, clad in some costume that is deemed really right for
her, to display before her teachers and her peers how well
she has done her homework. "At graduation," says the spokesman, "each girl gets a hatbox with basic beauty needs in it.
We also give each a lipstick, but only [emphatically, now]
with the complete understanding that it is not to be used without the parents' permission." The course, she reports, is a
bewitching success. "The girls just adore it. It is always filled
to capacity. The mothers are most enthusiastic, which is very
encouraging to us all, because, you see, we really believe in
this thing so strongly.

"I think one change we may try soon is treating this group

more like we do the older girls, bringing in celebrities to lecture them on charm and so forth. Some of them have complained that we treat them too much like children."

While educational institutions normally do not hand out charm diplomas or furnish beauty tips to preschoolers, let no one assume the wee ones are being ignored. They, too, are getting an education; the method is simply less direct. For example, a modern toy doll, a technological triumph of paint, permanent wave, and secondary sex characteristics, is a fine educational tool for indoctrinating preschoolers in the mystique of *haute couture*. In times past the dolls that sold best cried "Mama" more piteously than the competition, or wetted in exotic new ways; nowadays nothing means more to a little girl than owning the best-dressed doll on the block, and physiology be damned. A section on dolls' clothing figured prominently in an exhaustive research study drawn up, a while back, for one of the big guns in the doll-manufacturing business. Reporting on the appeals of a doll positively abloom with sexual maturation, the researchers stated that mothers initially objected to its figure but ultimately were won over by its *soigné* wardrobe. One mother who considered the doll too sexy for comfort changed her mind when her daughter said, "She is so nicely groomed, Mommy."

Thus, what *Vogue* and *Harper's* do for the insecure adult, a doll can do for the five-year-old, and if she doesn't know the difference between mink and muskrat by the time she is six (the chic doll, nowadays, comes equipped with its own stole), it is not for lack of opportunity to learn.

Most children do know, of course. Sophisticated elementary schoolers are well enough versed in fashion precepts to be able to tell at a piercing glance who is wearing the right label and who the copy. A famous high-style designer, who, like so many of her colleagues, has recently extended her vistas to the creation of children's clothes ("Such a challenge!"), has observed with pleasure, "These youngsters are adorable. They are so fantastically competitive, just like grown women. My little girl (age eleven) absolutely refuses to wear the same dress to school two days in a row. She has her wardrobe organized on a weekly basis, with a Monday dress, a Tuesday dress, and so forth, hanging next to each other in her closet. One morning she had a fit because her Friday dress was too small and she had nothing clean to take its place. She didn't want to go to school. I said, 'Nobody has a different dress for every day.' And she said, '*No*body? Mother, *every*body! We all keep track of each other, and no one ever, ever, ever wears the same dress to school twice in one week.'

"I have a dear friend in this business who designs less expensive things than I do. She gave my daughter two dresses as a birthday present, two of her own designs, and the child won't wear them. She is afraid the other girls will recognize them, because they are in all the department stores, and will know that she is wearing cheaper clothes." (Mystified, but not unpleasantly, the lady digresses to explain that she began designing for children because she thought they deserved something tastier than what was on the market—"All those eternal dirndls and overdone party dresses. I designed a party dress that I'm crazy about, a simple little thing made out of sari fabric, absolutely uncluttered, nothing to it." $75.) "They sound so adult, these children. I don't know where they get it. My daughter told me a little girl said to her, 'That color doesn't do a thing for you.' And she said, right back, 'You shouldn't wear plaid. You're too fat.' "

Almost as adorably, one third-grader retreated home to lick her wounds after having been blackballed from a secret sorority because she didn't own enough sweaters. "She was heartbroken," recalls the mother, herself markedly depressed. "I said, 'But, Josie, you have twelve sweaters.' She said, 'No I don't. Five of them are cardigans. You wear them open, so they don't count.' I said, 'So button them, and then they'll be sweaters.' She said, 'You don't button cardigans. Nobody buttons cardigans.' I said, 'Why not?' and she just looked at me and said, 'Oh, God.'

"I had to buy her some more sweaters, which she didn't need. It's a great expense, keeping up with all these chic kids. I've suggested to the other mothers that we crack down, and everyone says that's a fine idea, but no one does anything about it."

Why not? Why, despite the manifest disadvantages, do so many of the young look so frighteningly chic? The fashion-conscious mother is apt to explain that high style is essential to her offspring's morale. Other interested observers may claim that fancy clothes will do little for a child's morale, but a great deal for her mother's. "A well-dressed little girl," says a designer, speaking unofficially but from the heart, "enhances her mother's appearance. She complements the parent as effectively as a pearl necklace or a poodle. The well-groomed woman knows that every detail is important, including her child."

But the prevailing authoritative, which is to say analytical, view holds that something more than décor is involved, as revealed by an analyst who was asked recently whether mothers ever use their children—purely in the fashion sense—as status symbols. "Do mothers," he replied wearily, "ever *not* use their children as status symbols?"

In his view, a heavy emphasis upon clothing is simply another way of using the child to express one's station in life. "She is *wearing* the child, you might say. When mama starts redecorating for a social climb, look out: she'll redecorate everything in sight, including—*especially* including—the children."

This leads to the question of whether high fashion is good or bad for children, and mothers, child worshipers and otherwise, disagree violently. Those who still retain the maverick spirit tend to go heavily sociological, attributing to early fashion training the high incidence of divorce, the high rate of homosexuality ("Making them wear those short pants and yum-yum haircuts. I mean, no *wonder!*,"), the low-protein content of the National Character, and other such dismal phenomena.

"This chic business is simply awful," says one such mother. "A little girl shouldn't look like a clotheshorse. She shouldn't think it's the end of the world if she can't get a new pair of shoes to match her dress. She shouldn't be competing with other little girls, and if she does you can be sure it's because her mother is competing with other big girls. If she has a $50 dress when she's five she will want a $500 dress when she's eighteen. And what if she grows up and marries a man who can't afford all that stuff? She'd make him miserable."

"Rich little girls seldom grow up to marry poor boys," counters a member of the opposition with seemingly irrefutable logic. "Besides, there's nothing wrong with a $100 dress for a child if the mother can afford it. She may make her daughter feel far less self-conscious than the mother who spends $5 and keeps nagging the child, 'Don't get your dress dirty' because she can't afford a maid to wash it.

"I think even the mother of limited means owes it to herself and to her child to teach the child how to be well dressed and to dress her *as stylishly as she can possibly afford*. After all, fashion is one of the things that makes ladies and gentlemen."

This is substantially at odds with the view taken by Miss

Amy Vanderbilt, taste arbiter in the post–Emily Post era and
no woman to take her responsibility lightly. "A high-priced
dress for a little girl is an abomination," she says simply. "It is
parvenu. A lady—even a *little* lady—should wear gloves to
protect her hands, of course, and she shouldn't be allowed on
the street looking sloppy or dirty. But all this high-fashion
business sets bad values. If I had a daughter she would be
plainly, inexpensively dressed and she wouldn't be allowed
to set foot in a chi-chi store until she was twenty. I do not
think that women of the ten-best-dressed variety are very
happy or fulfilled women."

However ladies of the ten-best-dressed variety may feel
about the matter, child psychiatrists are agreed on the following points: first, that the mother who needs to make her
child into a fashion plate feels emotionally insecure, particularly with other women; and secondly, that using one's
child to bolster one's ego is playing dirty pool with the budding
personality.

"There are two ill effects," says one. "First, the child *feels*
used. She feels the compulsion to conform or her mother won't
love her. And then, she senses her mother's feelings of inferiority. She may become plagued with these feelings herself
and go all out to impress others with her outer appearance ("A
cardigan is *not a sweater!*" cries the little reject), while in-
wardly she feels that if people really knew her they wouldn't
like her at all."

Relenting somewhat, the doctor concedes that a woman
doesn't always strive for the Best-Dressed, senior and junior
divisions, simply because of an inferiority complex. She may
be merely spoiled ("*Recently* spoiled, I should say. Although
again you get much the same kind of anxiety neurosis: she's
in a bracket she's not accustomed to and that makes her feel
insecure so she compensates wth her clothes and her children

and all her other accessories"), or she may be bored, lonely, frustrated ("Plain women eat; chic women buy"). In either case, apparently, the prospects are dim for her offspring.

Does salvation, then, lie in blue jeans?

"Not at all," says another psychiatric man. "The parent who says, 'Go on, put on these jeans and roll on the floor so people will *know* I'm liberal'—that parent is simply enslaved by another set of mores."

This doctor has a strong notion that it is possible to tell a good bit about mothers from the way they dress their children in relation to themselves. If the child is dressed elegantly and the mother plainly, for example, she is likely to be an overly self-sacrificing type who shoves the maid aside to slave over a hot stove and otherwise makes life difficult for her family. Her only jewels are the jewels of Cornelia; they are always dressed to kill, while she provides the perfect foil in simple black.

If both mother and child are consistently dressed beyond her means, she is plumping for status. "A patient of mine always used to go into expensive stores, take designer dresses into the dressing room, and rip out the labels. Then she would sew them into her own clothes," he says. "But with her daughter, she had a problem: there is a very high-class brand of children's clothes that I gather is a big taste symbol among the mothers; if the kid wears this particular company's clothes it shows you're *au courant*. But she couldn't steal the labels from *those* clothes and sew them into cheaper things, because these mothers know every garment the company manufactures and would spot a phony.

"One day she came in elated. She had found a discount house that carried factory rejects of this merchandise—a seam sewn crooked, a sleeve cut too short, nothing you would notice much. Real bargains, she said. So she started making expeditions to the discount house to buy these clothes in any sizes they had, and then she would take them into regular department stores and say she'd gotten them as gifts and wanted to exchange them for the right size. The daughter ended up with the right label and the right size and perfect seams and sleeves, and everything was rosy.

"We spent several sessions discussing this quirk of hers, and for what it cost her to work the thing through she could have bought the stuff at the regular price and had money to spare."

If the child is always poorly attired and the mother unfailingly chic, she is either competitive with her young one or simply not much interested. And the competitive mother may have reason to be, for her daughter most certainly is; in this regard the doctor settles—for all time, one might hope— the question of for whom females dress. A widely accepted lay theory holds that preschool girls dress to please their mothers, school girls to look like their friends, and post-school girls to impress their enemies. Wrong, our man says. A little girl dresses not for her mother or siblings or friends or even herself, but for her daddy. And he finds no reason to doubt that she goes on dressing to please men, primarily, all the rest of her life.

And a final point: "Actually, the mother's motives are far more important than what the child wears. Fancy clothes won't do a child any harm at all. But the mother who buys them may. Oh, yes indeed."

As doctors continue to ponder the dark import of pint-sized fashion, the training bras sell on; one lingerie manufacturer even was forging ahead, recently, with a dynamic scheme to make them in black. The fashion magazines continue to sing their *soigné* songs ("For the envy of her kindergarten class: this French import in a burnt-umber velveteen, its line sweeping cleanly from a sparse little yoke, pure shape, pure Female . . ."). The ranks of fashion-happy mothers press forward, bearing their chic charges before them like escutcheons. And the young elegants themselves move blithely to the forefront, their ids solid, their egos secure, and their fancies conjuring up visions of a new season filled with devastating new shapes, divine new colors, and the latest word from Paris.

"Yes, I like the olive shades," said a ten-year-old recently, speaking in tones of eminent reason. "I also like red, blue, and beige. I don't like frills of any sort. I prefer simple, sophisticated things, like tight skirts and good fabrics and low necks if I want to wear jewelry. No, I don't have a bra. I'm the only girl in my class who doesn't have one. My mother thought it was important because it would keep me from sagging later, but my father wouldn't let her buy me one. He is very old-fashioned. I liked plaid when I was younger but I don't anymore. I got shoes with little heels for my tenth birthday. I wear them to parties and I will get higher heels for my eleventh birthday. White gloves are a nuisance but I always wear them when I get dressed up. When I was four my mother's friend in Texas sent me a mink skin with a note that said, 'I wanted to be sure you got your first mink from me.' I wore it then, because it was gay, but I wouldn't wear it now because fur is cheap-looking at my age. Of course, I will enjoy wearing fur later on. I am also looking forward to wearing lipstick. No, I am not looking forward to my first black dress. I have been wearing black since I was three, and to tell the truth, I am sick and tired of it."

AT CAMP

Snakebite Is Not the Problem

It is noted in lesser annals of the national saga that organized camping for children began just a mite over a century ago, in 1861. Founding father and spiritual leader of summer camping was one Frederick W. Gunn, a Yale man, whose inspiration it was to hitch several boys to a wagon and a cow, thereby insuring a fresh supply of milk, and blaze a trail into the wilds of Milford, Connecticut, where they set up a campsite. "Gypsying," it was called in those days. Mr. Gunn might be at a loss to know what to call it now.

Among professional camping people it is no idle question, having split their ranks and poised them upon the sharp edge of an agonizing reappraisal: What, they ask—eying the $1,000 tuitions, the torrid pursuit of Culture, the gentle amenities of plumbing, screening, and innerspring mattresses—what the devil *is* camping in these splendidly appointed times?

For one thing, it is a half-billion-dollar industry, embracing some fifteen thousand camps that minister to five and a half million children. For another, it is an industry that has increased a hundredfold since the end of World War II—reasonably enough, the same period during which large numbers of children seem to have learned more and more about how to do less and less of anything that doesn't take money or organization.

Most of the camps in operation today are agency or institutional affairs, run by everyone from the Boy Scouts and Camp Fire Girls to the Salvation Army, the Y.M.C.A.'s, and a heavy clutch of school and church organizations. They may pamper their young more than did the camps of former days, but by and large they are devoted and dedicated institutions, low- or no-profit, offering the outdoor life, for which they have a respect akin to awe, to millions of youngsters who otherwise might never know the joys of nature.

But the hard, elite core that we concern ourselves with here —the sweet summer promise awaiting the stripling who, having spent himself in a long, hard winter of overprivilege, so clearly deserves a rest—is the private camps.

Almost a million children attend the privates. Costs range roughly from $500 for the eight-week season, which is modest in the extreme, to $1,000, exclusive of laundry, Polaroid film, riding lessons, and other incidentals. As with the schools, the longest waiting lines form in front of the most expensive, exclusive camps, and the competition for entrance is almost as keen.

However, the most striking characteristic of these camps is not their cost but what they offer for the money. Today there is a camp to meet the specific desires and requirements of almost any mother's child from six to sixteen who ever deserved, in one way or another, the very best.

There are camps that specialize in sailing, water-skiing, basketball, baseball, tennis, golf, horseback riding (riding camps are broken down into several subspecies: cross-country, saddle-seat, hunt seat, rodeo, stable management and horse care); camps that specialize in modern dance, in drama, in chamber music, in oil painting, in conversational French (including French Manners and How to Read French Menus), and other respectable enrichments; camps for fat children ("sailing, sports, cultural activities, subtly combined with diet control"—a brochure), thin children, shy children, over-achievers, underachievers, and several other categories of problem children. There are work and farm camps, which enjoy a limited but highly enthusiastic following by virtue perhaps of their sheer novelty. For the kiddie who has been around and requires something really different, there are always the camps that specialize in pre-flight training.

But the most inevitable product of its time is the school camp, an institution whose growth rate nicely approximates that of the mounting college hysteria. In a school camp, only a part—the lesser part—of each day is devoted to recreation. The rest is schoolbooks. Nor are these vacation spas necessarily for backward children or, as the euphemism has it, "slow learners." The New England woods (it is there, in the Ivy League climate, that school camps proliferate) are full of brainy youngsters hell-bent for Harvard, and forging ahead four seasons a year to beat out the competition.

Camp directors who recall with nostalgia the days when a gong mustered campers to nothing more intellectually demanding than blueberry picking, are notably cool to the school camps. "They have taken the 'camp' out of camping," one says. But theirs is a minority viewpoint. The head of a school and camp advisory service reports that of four hundred camps in her files, more than half now offer some kind of scholastic instruction. "They have to," she says, "or the school camps will leave them with empty bunks. The parents I talk to aren't much concerned with leather tooling anymore. They want camps that will help prepare their kids for the college entrance boards. They want a cultural approach, too. They are crazy for camps with a cultural approach."

Thus given their mandate, the camps now push scholastic tutoring and cultural courses as prime attractions. Where camp advertisements in the Sunday supplements once stressed safe waterfronts and sound protein diets, headlines now proclaim: "Oil Painting Lessons by Professional Artist!"—"A Practical Study Course Including French, Spanish, Russian and Journalism"—"Optional Summer Session, Tutoring, Remedial Reading, Professional Testing Guidance"—"All Water Sports, Plus the Disciplines of Fine Arts and Intellectual Stimuli."

"I never thought I'd be hiring a French teacher for my campers," says one old-timer, bowed down by wealth and compromise. "But the customers want it. They love it, their baby comes to us for eight weeks and then he goes home and says, 'Bonjour, mama,' they're the envy of the neighborhood. Gives us a certain class, you know. It sure as hell isn't camping, but it *is* class.

"Before the season starts, these mothers ask me, 'What cultural advantages will my child have? Do you teach madrigal singing?' If I say we do not, she says, 'Oh, I really do want her to learn madrigal singing. My friend's daughter learned it at such-and-such a camp last summer and she was *so* happy there.' Then I say, 'But *she* didn't learn conversational French, did she? *Your* daughter will learn conversational French!' It can go on like that for hours before you get them to make a deposit."

The subliminal considerations that intrude here are, of

course, considerable. In the view of one man with twenty years' experience, many parents pick a camp to suit their own needs rather than those of the children. "They may say they're doing it because it's a healthy life for the children, but you don't see them giving any business to the Boy Scout camps." Those who pack a child off to some plush camp while they themselves laze by the country club pool have a twofold motive. First, they have their own position to maintain. A child in the wrong camp, when their friends' children are in the right one, may reflect poorly upon them. Secondly, they want to get rid of Junior, who in the absence of his buddies must be kept amused. The urgent desire to let somebody else amuse him gives rise to a certain guilt, our man says, which they assuage by seeking out the poshest camp they can find— one that extends "every advantage."

"When I go out to interview the family, I hear the mother tell the child, 'This is your vacation, darling. You don't have to go to camp unless you want to.' Then she tells me, 'I hope he decides to go. He'll be bored to death hanging around the house all summer.' What she means is, she'll have him on her neck all summer.

"Most of these kids live in nice homes, with plenty of lovely, open play space around. But still they are sent to camp so they won't spend the summer nagging their mothers for something to do. It's easier to hand them a $100-a-week vacation for eight weeks than teach them how to entertain themselves."

And what constitutes the "right" camp? Here opinions diverge wildly. According to one woman who has been running a camp information bureau for many years, it depends on what set of conformities the parents salute.

"Generally we find that parents who have never been to camp themselves, or perhaps have acquired their money only recently, are anxious to place their childen in the luxury camp —what we call the country club camp, if you can call it a camp at all. They want their youngsters to go where the kids from socially prominent families go. They want the sports that are fashionable—golf, tennis, riding—that sort of thing. And, of course, they want a program in the arts.

"Such parents do not want their children sleeping in tents. They demand every physical comfort. One mother once requested a camp with air-conditioned cabins. I told her that in camping we have what is called natural air-conditioning.

"Then there are the parents who are somewhat more progressive, more avant-garde—the people who drive old cars and dress their children in old clothes. They wouldn't let their kid be caught dead in a country club camp, they consider it gauche. They want him in a camp with more rugged facilities, and they always ask a great many questions about the philosophy of the camp and whether there is a psychologist on staff. They are all for a cultural program, of course, but they want square dancing instead of ballroom dancing and real folk music instead of campfire songs. Many people who used to request luxury camps are now looking for camps that rough it. They have learned it's less provincial. So far as I'm concerned, it's just a different kind of snobbism, that's all. People want their children to go to the kind of camp that reflects the image they have of themselves."

Those whose self-image tends to Grande Baroque find no dearth of camps to mirror it. For this clientele the camps themselves trade heavily in snob appeal. They exude social position, suggesting in brochures the need for a child to have worthy peer relationships, and many print rosters of socially prominent customers on their stationery. One camp uses an ingenious application form. Where the applicant is to fill in his name there appears the customary "Mr. and Mrs. ———"

and, directly below, "Dr. and Mrs. ———" Aha! Professional people send their children here!

To reinforce the aura of desirability, one camp owner, who has more business than he can handle anyway, sends out "invitations" to the children he deems acceptable—*after* the personal interviews, rather like a private school dean or a sorority president. "It works like a charm," he says. "The kids who don't get invitations are crushed. I've had mothers call me, mad as hell, demanding to know why their children weren't accepted."

For parents who respond to this kind of appeal, what matter money? The higher the fee, the more desirable the camp. "Many people are more concerned about what they pay for the camp than about its quality," says a placement director. "If we recommend a camp that is modestly priced, they won't even consider it. They say it probably wouldn't be 'good enough' for their child. We recommend it because we feel it would be perfect for the child. But I guess it wouldn't be perfect at all for the parents."

In this regard there is the grievous experience of one woman who sent her son to a new camp of the country club variety, sight unseen. The child had a dreadful summer and came home complaining of bad food and incompetent counselors, charges substantiated by other campers. His mother passed the complaints on to an official of the Association of Private Camps. "But why did you send the child there without investigating the place?" he asked. "Well," the lady said, "my husband and I heard about it through a friend who makes the camp uniforms. When he told us how much the shirts were going to cost, we figured any place that would put children into shirts that expensive *must* be a good camp."

Camps of this ilk tend to be so well groomed and manicured

that a child can make the transition from home painlessly and, indeed, need hardly feel he is away. As one observer has pointed out, "It is more like being in a summer resort without wall-to-wall carpeting."

This isn't precisely so, the fact being that there now *are* camps with wall-to-wall carpeting; in recent seasons a number of knowledgeable entrepreneurs have taken to buying up old luxury hotels and converting them into camps. The conversion is not conspicuous. In several of these establishments toddlers brave the elements from semiprivate rooms with bath and telephone. "The most exciting innovation in young people's vacations!" reads one brochure, noting further, with a commendably candid use of quotation marks which in all fairness should not go unnoticed, that children " 'camp' at a luxury resort hotel. They eat in the hotel's main dining room and sleep in guest accommodations. . . ." Other literature, less disposed to call a spade a spade, offers "two months of ideal camp life" in a former country club.

But country club camping does not necessarily presuppose country club facilities. On a traditional camping site, in cabins equipped with nothing more pretentious than screens and indoor plumbing, the living can be swish indeed. What was, in long-gone camp parlance, a recreation hall may be called a "little theater" or a "drama workshop." The drama staff may include a set designer and a costume designer, and the show that parents see on visiting day is no homegrown revue but a grand-scale production of some Broadway musical (*My Fair Lady* and *The Sound of Music* have been enjoying great favor in recent seasons). Sometimes there may be bowling alleys— an item that turns traditionalists blue with fury—on the grounds; and replacing such quaint classics as copper hammering, Indian lore, and those braided whistle chains of yesteryear, fashioned in camp colors and lovingly wrought at the arts-and-crafts bench to be presented to one's counselors, are water-skiing, scuba diving, and judo.

In co-ed camps, evening "socials" are a main attraction, and the belles-in-training are wont to spend their days preparing for their nights. (One mother vividly recalls visiting her ten-year-old daughter to find the child out on the tennis courts with her bunkmates, bouncing balls about languidly, hair up in curlers and lipstick gleaming wetly in the noonday sun. The next summer she scoured the placement agencies and came up with an all-girls' sailing camp on Cape Cod. "But, mother," said the wee one, now eleven, "what will I do in the *evenings?*") "We have a hard time getting the girls into the water," says a director, "because they're afraid of spoiling their hair. They sit on the dock in pin curls." The solution, possibly, would be to do away with socials, but the man wants to stay in business. One camp has licked the problem by adding a full-time hairdresser to its staff; a loudspeaker summons girl campers to their appointments.

Some of the camps book entertainers, just as adult resorts do. Not any old third-rate comedian, either; the youngsters have been around the TV channels, and they are fussy. "You have to entertain them in style," says a counselor, "or they won't be back next season."

Country club camping is comfortable camping. Where the intrepid Frederick Gunn and his wilderness boys went forth with only a cow, today's overnight sojourns into the woods, commonly known as "tripping," are veritable safaris. One camp goes tripping with a station wagon full of supplies in tow. They don't stray far from home, either; some don't stray at all. "An overnite outdoor camping site is available *on the grounds,* whereby campers are provided the opportunity for 'real camping,' " one advertisement reads. Of course, the activity is optional. "Some parents absolutely forbid it," says a camp spokesman. "They're afraid of snakes. Actually, our problem is kids, not snakes. I have found that a child who can sleep soundly in a big city, with all the traffic noises right outside his window, will wake up and fall apart when a twig crackles in the woods."

Other camps have frequent "Indian cook-outs." Translation: several counselors and an aggregation of Bermuda-shorted young bloods trodding a well-worn warpath to a barbecue pit, closely followed by a chuck wagon full of steaks and the camp chef. "Our parents like the *appearance* of ruggedness without the hardship," says an old Indian cook-out hand. "They think our chuck wagon routine is wonderful."

Most professional camp people do prefer the old-fashioned brand of camping. Though their rustic standards may have fallen before the tide of parental pressures ("I installed hot showers, I hired a music teacher," one says doggedly, "but I *will not build an indoor pool*"), they would like to believe that the old pioneering spirit lingers, latent, in their luxury-drugged clientele. Dreamers. A study of some four hundred boys made by a camp owner to determine what they wanted most from camping revealed the following: They rated inter-camp competition low, overnight camping lower yet, vigorously nixed nature study, and evidenced a massive indifference to the importance of developing good sportsmanship.

Other, less exhaustive studies indicate that what campers, age ten and up, feel *is* important, is the camp's philosophy on such matters as going steady and necking. At a camp directors' convention, one conflicted party reported on the findings, hardly earthshaking, of a study he had undertaken among campers. "New social habits have developed," he said. "Girls of eleven and twelve years of age start to use lipstick, smoke, date and 'go steady.' Either because of neglect or the so-called 'liberal' or 'permissive' attitude on the part of parents, the children have complete freedom at home. These youngsters consider it perfectly proper to hold hands anywhere, kiss and neck privately or in public. Often, they expect to do these things without staff restraint in the camp."

Some campers, he continued, cared little for any phase of the camp program other than the evening soirées. "Their chief interest was the big dance, and they preferred to rest, primp, and prepare for it. . . ."

What to do? What would Old Camper Gunn have done? These are not, like snakebite and missing laundry, classic camping problems, and the camp directors were stumped. In the soul-searching talk that followed, one man reduced the problem to its most pragmatic application: "Here are a group of boys and girls at a social," he said. "They are dancing, the juke box is playing, they are having a wonderful time. And let us even assume that they are not dancing cheek to cheek and that they are doing the sort of things that you, as a camp director and as a parent, would approve of.

"Now comes the end of the social. . . . Do the boys walk the girls to the entrance of the girls' cabins? Do you permit a good-night kiss? How long should that good-night kiss go? These are real, practical questions, because they are the things the kids are going to pick you up on. 'Is it wrong? We do the same thing in the city, our parents know about it. Why should you try to stop us from doing the things that we do in the city that our parents know about?' "

Thus the dilemma that confronts a large segment of the camping world today. Parents are not necessarily any help. The child who has not, in the parental view, shown sufficient social aggressiveness in the city, is pushed harder in camp. "My child isn't getting enough social life," a mother wrote to one camp owner, after her daughter had telephoned home to complain she hadn't set the boys on fire at the latest dance. "Please see that she mixes more." ("If a kid is unpopular we get blasted by the mother," says a counselor. "It's never the child's fault, it's the camp's.") Even the six- and seven-year-olds may be encouraged to get in their social kicks—"although we do break these socials down by age, of course," a camp man adds hastily. "The small girls attend dances only with the small boys. It wouldn't be appropriate to have them mixing with the older groups in the evening."

To limit parental bird-dogging, many camps today allow only one or two visiting days a season. Few of them dare, however, to deny parents frequent telephone contact (one brochure notes: "We are equipped with an elaborate public-address and intercommunications system, and campers may receive calls at any time before Taps"), and this can breed its own headaches.

"An anxious mother doesn't have to be on the premises to ruin her child's summer," says one observer, a man of small patience with country club camping. "She calls up and says, 'Are you having a good time?' and the child says, 'Yes, great!' She says, 'Don't you miss me?' and the child says, 'Yes, I miss you.' She says, 'Are you *sure* you miss me? You don't *sound* like you miss me.' And before she's done the kid is bawling. Or she will write a letter about how she and daddy are so lonesome for him, and how his friend next door keeps asking when he is coming home, and how his poor doggie won't eat a thing because he misses him so much, and the child is thrown into a panic. I do love children, or I wouldn't have been able to *endure* them all these years, but I never have been able to reconcile myself to the fact that campers come with parents."

The anxious parent, he says, will set the summer's course at the very outset by showing up on the day of departure with a list of instructions for the counselor. This is generally a run-down on the child's idiosyncrasies, eating and sleeping habits, and of course his allergies. Our informant describes the scene:

"Here we are in the train station, with the timetable blaring away over the loudspeaker and thousands of kids milling around. We're trying to count noses, check baggage, get the bedlam organized, and meanwhile all these sobbing mothers are pushing instruction sheets into our hands and grabbing at our sleeves to ask last-minute questions. They ask the damnedest questions. 'How will my little girl sleep? She can't make a bed.' 'What if she has to get up and go to the bathroom and doesn't know the way?' 'How big is the mirror in the bathroom?' When we finally get the kids moving the last thing I hear, usually, is some mother hollering, 'And don't forget about Billy's allergy. . . .' Allergy, hell. You get Billy up to camp for a few days, give him some TLC but let him know you aren't about to lie down and die for him, and he gets along just fine. Half the time the only thing Billy is allergic to is his mother.

"Once we had this child arrive at camp with a shoebox full of pills and a yard-long instruction sheet from the mother. Our doctor and nurse decided to see how many of the pills the kid really needed. They cut them out, bit by bit, until he wasn't taking any. He thrived, he said he felt wonderful. When he got home his mother told us how great he looked, and then she put him right back on the pills again.

"We have had children come to camp with instructions not to let them swim, sit in the sun, or indulge in any strenuous sports. God knows what they come for. Of course, you can't say they don't get anything out of it. Instead of hiking they get music. Instead of nature study they get science: ham radio operating and electronics. I suppose that's okay, but it's not camping. And the worst of it is, *this is what they want.*"

In marked contrast is the spirit at the so-called wilderness camps, where a boy knows or soon learns how to survive if he should ever find himself stuck without plumbing. There are not many wilderness camps—no more than 2 per cent of all the camps in the country, it has been estimated, still manage to hold firm against electricity—but the few extant are very fashionable with a limited public.

The guiding philosophy of these camps is that most children would really rather live dangerously, if only parents and television announcers would leave them alone. The camps are usually deep in the woods, with minimal facilities—outhouses, simple dining hall, and tents or log cabins, open-fronted to admit no barrier to nature's creatures ("If a boy can't stand a couple of mosquito bites, what kind of a man is he going to be, anyway?"). The campers chop their own wood, cut their own ice, wash their own clothes, and oftentimes bake their own bread and harvest vegetables from their own garden—organic, naturally. They do a great deal of swimming, canoeing and overnight hiking through rough terrain, carrying their own supplies. Their crafts are on the highbrow side—weaving, ceramics, pottery-making. They study flora and fauna, which would strike the country club camper as a curious occupation, and sometimes they even bird-watch. Their social lives, far from the savage beat of the cha-cha-cha, are unblushingly wholesome. They have treasure hunts. They discuss world affairs. There is generally a guitar on the premises, and in the evening they sit about a campfire singing folk songs and roasting marshmallows.

"Challenging work projects" are a strong feature of wilderness camping. The children clear trails, make steps, build bridges across brooks. This is not, of course, everyone's idea of a treat. The director of one such Spartan stronghold tells of a lad who balked at being assigned to build a fence. "I am not here to work," the newcomer said forthrightly. "I am here because my mother and I need a rest from each other." "Everybody works here," the director said. "How much are you paying?" the boy asked. "Nothing," the director said. The tyke whistled loudly. "Boy," he said, "you really got some racket here. My folks are paying *you* to let *me* build your crummy fence." And he may have had a point, at that.

Certainly, it is an expensive fence. The simple camp, like the simple black dress, costs plenty, and a parent has to be at least moderately well heeled to indulge his child in the illusion of poverty. "After all," explains a wilderness spokesman, "it is much more expensive to run our kind of camp. One man can handle eighteen boys on a ball field, but someone has to keep an eye on a kid with an ax."

For the parent who patronizes such camps, just as for his country club counterpart, price is secondary. "Parents who have entrusted their offspring to such a wild and wooly place," reads a promotion leaflet, in what is clearly a Bronx cheer to camps of more gentle persuasion, "are a rather special breed: they must approve of simplicity and ruggedness; they can at least understand ideals that may run counter to accepted custom. They enjoy ideas more than ostentation, the stimulus of alert minds more than the quest for status." To belong to this "special breed" connotes, of course, a status of its own. It is an exclusive society whose members empathize instinctively, rather like sports car owners flashing signals of *Gemütlichkeit* on the highway.

There is much talk among camp people about "progressivism," a matter they generally can argue better than they can define. When the subject comes up, the fancy-camp owner tends to hedge; the wilderness men, on the other hand, look a mother in the eye and tell her they are as progressive as anybody around, and maybe more so. Predictably enough, most of the wilderness camps are nonsectarian, and a good many of them are interracial. Several have been accused, like the private schools, of bringing in a few "token" Negro children to capture the white customers who are looking for a truly "democratic" camp, a charge largely, but not altogether, unjustified. (The interracial factor is of prime importance to parents who support such causes and want their children to do the same, but it does hold its dangers for parlor egalitarians. One couple, members of many progressive, interracial clubs and organizations and outspoken proponents of the good fight in their community, came to a camp director with a dilemma: their eighteen-year-old son, a longtime camper now turned counselor, had fallen in love with a young Negro counselor-in-training and they wanted to be married. "How can we *stand* it?" cried the mother. "How will it *look?*" "You mean, how will it look if your son marries the girl?" said the director. "Heavens, no!" she wailed, truly shocked. "We'd never let him *marry* her. I mean, how will it look to our *friends,* breaking it up after all the things we've *stood* for all these years?")

The progressive nature of the wilderness camp embraces, further, "democratic action." At one camp each tent has an elected "Little Chief" who meets with the director ("Big Chief") at a weekly "powwow" (Indian terminology is strong in the wilderness camps), to work out "policies" (activity programs and disciplinary problems). Big Chief makes suggestions, and the Little Chiefs are free either to accept them or vote him down. "Our procedure stems from educational progressive ideals," the director says. "We respect our children as individuals. We believe in majority rule." And what if the Little Chiefs decide to go bowling? "Oh, well, if that is what they want, that is what they want. I would *hope* that they would have better taste."

A penchant for "democratic action" is, in fact, notable

throughout camping. What the wilderness camps practice out of conviction, the plush camps may practice out of impotence. Nonetheless, the country club camper gets his say, just as he does at home. "There are very few camps left today," says an official of the American Camping Association, "where a bugle blows and you've got to move." The modern camp, she says, tends to be "camper-centered," rather than "activity-centered" like the camp of old.

"In the old days there was a very specific program of activities and the children had to abide by it. Today we feel, with so many pressures on them during the school year, children should have a release during the summer, a chance to do what *they* want to do. So the group partakes of planning the daily program, and if some child doesn't want to go along with the majority, why, he can just lie on his bed and read. Our job is simply to suggest activities, without making the camper feel that he *has* to do any of them.

"The camper-centered program is ever so much nicer than the old kind. If a child doesn't want to go on a hike, for example, he can stay at home and the other children will bring back a report of what they saw. That way"—brightly—"nobody really misses anything. And the child who is antisocial and never wants to join up at all is soon brought into the group by group pressure. It is a tremendous social experience."

If the jargon sounds vaguely psychiatric, it is not mere chance. Far beyond skills, sports, or anything so rudimentary as fun, "social orientation and group adjustment" is the focus of camp life. Camp people, all of them, speak of "living experience," "outdoor experience," "camp experience"; of "group play," "group influence," "group adjustment." A respectable number of camps have professional psychologists on staff ("but you have to be careful how you present this to parents," one director says, "or they might get the idea the camp is for disturbed children"), and social workers abound.

At a mammoth convention of the American Camping Association, attended a while back by some three thousand camp owners, counselors, and other interested parties from almost every type of camp, the analytic ambience was instantly apparent. The program notes were juicy with psychiatric promise. The wood-choppers and the fence-builders flocked with the French teachers and the golf mentors to panels, seminars, and general sessions addressed by psychologists, pediatric psychiatrists, and a clutch of child guidance people from universities and research institutions.

Tirelessly, for five long days (interrupted, at one point, by a resoundingly successful cook-out in Central Park, at which the Boy Scouts showed everybody a thing or two about pre-psychiatry camping), they parsed the Unloved Child, the Different Child, the Overt and Covert Leader, the Techniques of Open-End Staff-Child Planned Programs. Talk of traumas and conflicts rose upward like campfire smoke. The speakers and chairmen simply led the chorus; everyone from Camp Chico-Wa-Wa to the Salvation Army knew the lyrics by heart.

In one discussion group, attention turned to the Child Manipulator. "How do we handle this type?" asked a listener wearing a 4-H Club badge. "He doesn't genuinely relate, yet he exerts tremendous power over the group."

"How about that?" said the chairman. "How can we work through the group to harness the powers of the manipulator?"

A Salvation Army lady stood up shyly. "He is an emotionally underprivileged child, and a very hostile child," she suggested. "He may be overindulged at home, but he is not getting enough love and attention. He manipulates to attract attention. You can successfully give it to him by bringing him *into* the group. . . . Utilize his greater skills . . . and you can effect a cure."

Simultaneously forging ahead in another meeting room, a speaker addressed herself to the problem of Discipline. "I think that there is a sanctity of the body. It should never be hit. The punishment should be firm, but moderate: perhaps depriving the child of canteen privileges for several days. And when the punishment is over, the child should be made to feel he is just as loved as all the others. Prolonged rejection can be severely traumatizing. The child should feel, 'He punished me, but he loves me now.' "

When the five days were over, a visitor, exhausted and unspeakably impressed, made bold to ask a top convention official how it was that so many souls so lavishly laced with psychiatric know-how had been drawn to the once-simple art of camping. "Oh, but they haven't!" she said. "We're working on it, but we still have far too many people in camping who don't know *anything*. This is a beginning! Only a beginning!"

And what was the goal? "Why, to try to understand the child's problems, and help him work them through, so that he will be able to make a better adjustment to his social environment. I mean, if we can't do that, what is camping *for?*" Good question.

Not all the high ground is held, however. There are still camps that accept a good child without wondering if he is repressed, and camps that discipline a bad child (there are none, of course, in Boys Town camps) without wondering if he will crack up. There have even been indications, in the past couple of seasons, that "competition," long a dirty word in some camping quarters, is on its way back.

One camp placement adviser reports a Small Trend away from co-ed camps and toward "brother-and-sister" establishments—camps located close together, under joint or harmonious ownership, that maintain a separation of the sexes except for dances and other intermural events. Even the young concede certain advantages here. "If you go to a co-ed camp," an eleven-year-old veteran points out, "and there aren't any decent boys around, or the other girls get boys and you don't, you're stuck. This way, everyone is in the same boat. Besides, we see boys in the city all the time. We can get along without them for two months. Absence makes the heart grow fonder."

And as for the trend toward back-to-nature camping, the country-clubbers are not yet losing any sleep about it. Nonetheless, they find monumentally offensive the notion that the Smart Set is turning its back on hot and cold running water.

"It's a pose, that's all it is," one proprietor says angrily. "This wilderness business is a very artificial life. After all, we are in the twentieth century. Our children are in the twentieth century. *Our kind of camping* is in the twentieth century. We are creative. We are—progressive. Twenty-five years ago a camp was simply a place providing an outdoor experience for children. Today it is so much richer than that. It is a social, cultural, intellectual experience. *These* are the important values. What value is there in going out of your way to make a child uncomfortable? Why should he sleep on a cot if he can have a good mattress? Why should he have to crawl around with a kerosene lamp if he can have electricity? Why should his parents sit home, worried sick about him, if they can reach him in his cabin by telephone? Face it: Modern plumbing is a great innovation. Why shouldn't our children enjoy the benefit of it? You call that status when a small child has to go stumbling out of his cabin in the middle of the night? You call that"—incensed, now—"SMART SET?"

A final breath, a final assault. "Our kind of camping is no more luxurious than camping ever was," he says, a hand sweeping out over the golf driving range that glistens greenly, the brick recreation hall bearing the legend "Off-Broadway," the ceramic-tiled swimming pool in which his charges, at the moment, are cavorting. "It is no more luxurious than it ever was. It is simply more *adequate.*"

Now, then: "Do you mean to tell me that all the great technological advances, all the advantages we have in this great land of opportunity, that all the centuries of work and progress were meant for this?—that *we should deprive our children?*"

ON VACATION
Saved by the Sitter

While the Good Camp loudly bespeaks the Good Parent, the family vacation can do the job better and possibly even cheaper. It combines the same obvious desire to give one's child advantages with the added virtue of Togetherness, neatly implying that really happy families take their fun *en masse*.

Therefore, it should—and does—follow that the family vacation package plan is having its finest hour. Children nowadays are going more places than the Bobsey Twins ever dreamed of. "We have never gotten so many queries about traveling with youngsters," says a man from the American Automobile Association. "People used to go on vacation to get away from the children. Now they plan their vacations around the children. It is a trend that we think will keep going strong for many years."

So, happily, do department-store buyers of travel equipment

for children, of which there is a dazzling proliferation. So do automobile dealers, who report station wagon sales still staunchly on the rise, a fact they attribute largely to the wagon's wonderful way with children; bucket seats are not for the child-centered. Hotel and motel keepers are extending, with varying degrees of inner grace, every courtesy of the house to record numbers of youngsters; highway restaurant managers are getting to know them better than they might like, and highway filling-station attendants, weary of handing over the rest-room keys to hordes of fledgling travelers, attest with feeling to their prevalence on the road.

As with the family home, so with the family vacation: the child engineers it. It is he who largely determines, at least by indirection, where the family will go, when it will go, how it will go, and what it will do when it gets there. "On the planning of vacations," Dr. Spock has noted, "the child's benefit is often given first consideration, the father's next, the mother's last. Perhaps this is inevitable, because if the children are out of sorts nobody has any fun. . . ." Though the good doctor makes so bold as to suggest that the child doubtless would survive an occasional reversal of the order, the idea has yet to catch fire in child-centered circles.

Overwhelmingly, the family that travels together travels in summer. By any number of reasonable criteria summer may be an abominable season for travel, but that is hardly the point. "You don't go when you want to go, you go when the kids can go," says a travel agent. "When school is out, then you go." But he also notes a growing trend in recent years, not only among the affluent, to shorten summer vacations and take time out in winter as well. Does this mean that more parents are starting to strike for a holiday of their own? "Heavens, no. It simply means that more kids are getting two vacations a year." (In Scarsdale, where, as has been noted, precious little happens that is For Adults Only, schoolchildren a while back had several extra days tacked onto their winter vacation period—ostensibly to permit more time to study for final exams, but *sub rosa* believed to be merely a face-saving concession to the migratory habits of Scarsdale's young, many of whom routinely went South for the holidays and routinely returned several days after school had resumed session.)

If the child determines when the family will vacation, he also determines what route it will take. "The family group usually travels by car, and that can be hard on the nerves if you don't do it just right," says our A.A.A. man. "The important thing to remember is, Children come first.

"People come in to get our help in planning a motor trip. They say they want the kids to really see the country, they want to get off the beaten track and follow the back-country roads. No fixed schedule, no advance reservations, they don't want to feel restricted, they say." He smiles, inviting the world to share the irony. "Well, the truth of the matter is, children *are* restricting. You can go wandering all over the map when you're alone, but when you're with children you have *got* to stick pretty close to those main highways, where there are plenty of restaurants and rest rooms and Coke machines. Otherwise you're asking for trouble.

"And you have got to travel at their pace, not yours. You can't decide to clock an extra hundred miles one day just because you feel like it, because maybe *they* won't feel like it. They get so restless, you know. You set out on a thousand-mile trip and before you've gone ten miles they want to know how much longer it's going to take."

To help parents cope with this and attendant problems, the A.A.A. issues a tip sheet entitled "Traveling with Children," which notes at the outset:

"A motoring vacation, more than anything else, gives parents and children a chance to play together, share new experiences and weld themselves into a closer family unit. Ideally, as the car heads out of town . . . all worries are left behind, and the only thoughts are of fun and relaxation in pleasant surroundings.

"Sadly, however, such vacation trips don't always measure up to expectations. Traveling with children exposes one to perils that can put a severe strain on the natural bonds of parental affection. . . ."

How, then, to sidestep such perils while playing together, sharing new experiences, and having fun and relaxation in pleasant surroundings? A.A.A.:

"One formula for making good time with youngsters aboard is to leave before dawn. The children can sleep in the car a few hours, giving you uninterrupted driving time. After breakfast you should have another period of easy driving before the children start getting restless. . . .

"Empty ice-cream or milk cartons come in handy in case of car sickness. A damp washcloth rolled in aluminum foil and kept in the glove compartment is useful for cleaning off sticky hands and faces. . . .

"For safety's sake, children should not be allowed to: sit in driver's lap; stand on or climb over seats; stick arms, heads or toys out windows; fiddle with car controls and ignition key. . . .

"The urge to turn from the wheel to reprimand wrestling, screeching children is sometimes overpowering, but can be disastrous while driving. Instead, pull over and stop. Just doing that often has a sobering effect. Such a situation is often a good signal for a break, anyway. . . ."

On the not inconsiderable question of how to keep children happy in a moving vehicle, the A.A.A. suggests playing games together, singing songs together, and breaking out some new toys when all else begins to pall. This problem of protecting the traveling child from boredom is one about which little was known until recently, perhaps because it was never considered a problem. Today, however, it engages the efforts of a good many researchers and has yielded up prodigious amounts of useful information. The subject of car games alone is large enough to constitute a book, and, in fact, does—Mr. Dave Garroway having seen fit to pen a work entitled, *Fun on Wheels: 150 Games, Puzzles and Brainteasers to Help Parents Keep Children Entertained and At Peace in the Car.* Adult pursuits may have to take a back seat to such *divertissements,* but as one mother points out in artful compromise, "It's really a matter of self-interest. You keep them entertained, they let you relax."

Having set the time and the pace, it follows that children set the destination. "They are very travel-conscious," a travel agent says. "Every September we start getting calls from children asking for maps of different places and wanting to know the best way to get there. They are already planning their summer itineraries. It's really something. I remember when I was a kid we used to love hearing about the places our parents had been. Now I think the parents go along for the ride.

"I had one little guy in here with his folks, they were planning a trip, and suddenly the kid says, 'I want to go to Arizona.' The parents ignore him, so he says again: 'I want to go to Arizona.' They're still ignoring him, see, and finally he gets red and says, real loud, 'I WANT TO GO TO ARIZONA.'

"Then the father says to him, 'I've already told you, mommy and I don't *want* to go to Arizona.' And the kid says, 'This is a democracy. Let's flip a coin.' So they flipped a coin and they went to Arizona." (Clearly a misinterpretation of due process, this. Had the parents held out for a vote apiece they could have won.)

Even when a child has no particular destination in mind he is a powerful deciding force. Wise parents, as another travel agent points out, go places where children will find things to enjoy other than the scenery. The shore is far better than the sweet serenity of yonder hills, and an Indian village infinitely snappier than the Grand Canyon, which, according to a vast body of parental research, should be covered fast.

Best of all is family camping, the Cinderella vacation, whose stupendous growth in the past decade never could have occurred without the vigorous support of children. It combines attractions for all but the most doggedly urban child with relative economy, an abundance of Togetherness, and, at this juncture, nearly all the comforts of home. This unique constellation of merits has won seventeen million disciples to date, and the trend grows. The only holdouts are mothers, many of whom apparently do not cotton to the good trailer-tent life.

"I hate it," says one mother, a survivor of three summers in the wilderness surrounded by plug-in hair-driers, collapsible cocktail shakers, and, framing every vista, a clump of cabin tents. "But the kids love it, and anything you *know* they like is easier on the nerves than trying something new."

This hard-core principle of family travel is aptly illustrated by the gripping experience of one New Jersey couple who forfeited the customary family week at the shore for a sentimental journey to Montreal. It seemed the parents had spent their honeymoon in Montreal and now were returning for their tenth wedding anniversary, bearing the sweet fruit of their union: two boys, age nine and eight.

"We started out at noon, after brunch," the father recalls grimly. "A half hour out the younger kid upchucked all over his brother and we stopped to mop them up. Then we got to a toll station and I let the big boy throw the only change I had into the Exact Change box and he missed, which held traffic up for quite some time. Then the kids got restless and wanted more funny books and I said they had plenty of funny books and my wife said, 'Let's play another car game,' and I said, 'I'm sick of those damn car games,' and she and I stopped talking and the boys started fighting. I reached back to separate them and almost crashed into another car and my wife screamed and we stopped for a snack.

"When we hit our motel it was almost dark and I had clocked 220 miles, seven stops, and four snacks. We got into our room—half-rate, you know, for kids under twelve when they stay with their parents; my God, who ever thought *that* one up! There we were, all four of us in this miserable room, and my wife and I couldn't fight and we couldn't make up. Happy anniversary.

"In the morning she and I talked it over and we said Goodbye, Montreal. We got back by noon, dropped the kids off at my brother's house and went to New York for a long weekend. Had a wonderful time."

Travel agents, who may recognize a professional duty to endorse the family vacation, are nonetheless a realistic bunch and some even leave their own children home when they travel, though they prefer not to brag about it. "This whole trend is a very mixed blessing," says one specialist of sorts in family package plans. "When you're with children you have to confine your activities to their level. The only alternative is to try to upgrade the children, and that can be a disaster. It really isn't fair to impose your taste on them."

Is there, as Dr. Spock in his infinite compassion has suggested, no small grain of equity in the reverse? How about the parent who would rather be elsewhere than, say, Disneyland?

The agent finds this very funny. "Oh, that's *different,*" she says, coming up with what may be the choicest definition yet of Togetherness: "Parents are *supposed* to enjoy seeing the children enjoy something, even if they don't really enjoy it themselves." A ruminating pause. Then: "My *personal* opinion is that vacationing with small children is just no vacation at all. It is hell."

Why, then, do people do it? Well, says the family package specialist, maybe there are a great many parents who travel with children simply because they really enjoy it, whatever the drawbacks; and a great many others who have nobody to take the brood gratis and can't afford a baby-sitter. "But I am not talking about them. I see women who put their children into private camp in July so they won't have them hanging around, and then pull them out of camp in August to go to some resort 'so we can all be together.' My customers tell me they need a vacation away from the children, and then they end up taking the vacation *and* the children. Don't tell me they're doing it just because they enjoy it. They're doing it because it would make them guilty if they didn't."

In her view, to count the children out produces remorse. To count them in, however, is desirable on several fronts: it makes one a virtuous parent; it makes one a popular parent, an important consideration; and it may even, praise be, make one a prestige parent, respected and envied by less adequate parents who have never, themselves, gotten the hang of family fun. Thus a back seat full of children is a perfect means of boosting one's image as the good captain of a grand crew. Is everybody happy? Well, no. There is still the problem of that inner self yearning for some respite from the wee ones.

Precisely this dilemma has led to a situation remarkably comparable to events in the homebuilding field, wherein fashionable parents now build two domains, junior and senior, under one roof. When these people travel, what they want is what they left back home: Togetherness with a strong dollop of apartheid.

"They tell me," says the travel agency lady, " 'Vacations are the only time we can all relax and really get to know each other,' and then ask me to find someplace where there are plenty of children's activities to keep the youngsters off their necks."

Thus, for those who want it, has come a new kind of family vacation whose spirit is strictly laissez-faire and whose symbol is the baby-sitter. All but the most laggard hotels and resort spots nowadays push baby-sitting services and special children's programs as prime attractions. "Have a glorious holiday *together*," reads one typical advertisement. "Our trained children's staff will keep the youngsters occupied while you golf, swim or just laze in the sun . . . Supervised meals in our Small-Fry dining room . . . Competent baby-sitters will take over while you dance under the stars . . ."

In a magazine article titled "Child-Centered Resorts . . . Boon to Vacationing Parents," a mother describes the holiday delights therein: "We visited a lovely old country hotel that has a complete day camp, staffed by expert counselors, which runs from nine in the morning to five in the afternoon, and again from six to eight, if the child is old enough. . . . For children under two, there are individual nursemaids at no extra charge. A resident pediatrician is on call at all times and has daily clinic hours. Not only was there a children's dining room, there were *three:* one for infants and toddlers, with high chairs, jars of baby and junior foods, and a refrigerator for formulas; one for camp-age children; and one for those who preferred to eat with Mommy. Ours was bewildered by the large camp dining room, so I sat with him in this cheerful, chintz-curtained room during mealtimes. It gave us a chance to visit."

As with so many innovations designed primarily for the comfort and stature of parents—the day camp, the dancing lesson, twin family rooms come to mind in passing—this one redounds mightily to the child's advantage. No family vacation plan, however it may please the parent, is going to work for long unless the child enjoys it, too. Thus the people who run Vacationland are faced with the fact that he who best serves children best serves himself, and they are vying stoutly to provide the service. The travel trails are ashimmer with ploys and gimmicks to keep the restless young contented while parents eat, sleep, and tan in peace. To lure the family trade, motels stock a modern arsenal: baby-sitters, wading pools, playgrounds, ping-pong tables, miniature golf courses. "It's expensive, and it's a damned nuisance," says a motel executive, "but what choice have we got? If we don't provide for the kids, somebody else will. This is the way things are today. If you can't keep up, you might as well go out of business."

"We've got a terrific setup here, a terrific setup," says another. "Anyone who registers here can leave the children with us for *hours* and go off without a worry. We have sandboxes and seesaws and games and a separate TV set for kids and a comic-book library. Now we are even thinking of installing a little theater, to show cartoons. We welcome children. We love having children. Pets, too. Children and pets," he says, stroking his cash register, "are our honored guests."

(In this regard, the once ubiquitous No Pets Allowed notice is becoming nigh extinct, as hostelry folk bow to the realization that when tykes travel Rover may not be far behind. So marked is this trend that the A.A.A. has seen fit to issue a booklet listing hotels and motels that are cordial to dogs, a sort of canine Duncan Hines.)

Enlightened restaurateurs are similarly solicitous of the juvenile trade. A favorite gambit is the Kiddie Cocktail, which does away with any archaic demarcation that may still exist between the Children's Hour and the Cocktail Hour. Designed to keep moppets from feeling neglected while adults chomp their martini olives, the Kiddie Cocktail is a ginger-ale concoction commonly known as a Roy Rogers when served to boys, a Shirley Temple when served to girls; it is generally swizzled compliments of the house, and smart waiters bring it to the table without being asked. Great, too, is the largesse of the numerous establishments that serve free ice cream to children under twelve. The Kiddie Menu is now almost common law, but many restaurants go it several paces better with free balloons and comic books for children waiting to be seated.

Many of the Howard Johnson restaurants, self-made sachems of the highways, provide coloring table mats with three crayons apiece, a service which can mess up the premises but apparently pays off in good will. "We are rapidly expanding our thinking along these lines," says a man from one of the chain's eateries. "Eventually we would like to have a small, supervised playground area just outside the restaurant, where the kids could work off their energies while parents finish their coffee and have a cigarette in peace. Many mothers have made that suggestion." Since the restaurant chain has virtually a captive clientele on many roads, this is pure *beau geste* and, as one mother has put it, darn nice of Howard Johnson.

While the genial bonifaces of the open road thus make life bearable for the child in transit, the big resort hotels make it truly gracious. (To be sure, there are still popular resorts that do little for children and couldn't care less; but they are wholly devoted to the aid and abetment of spouse-seekers, and therefore don't really count in this context.) That the resort hotels offer all sorts of special rates and package plans goes without saying; their real challenge is to keep the child happy, busy, and independent of his parents.

Most resorts meet it with a daily calendar of children's programs, parties, and lessons, all well supervised and geared to keeping the young occupied until bedtime. In places that really manage this sort of thing well, it is possible for children and parents to vacation together for a full twenty-four hours without a single direct confrontation. Many resorts have children's "clubs," which is a painless way of saying day camps, until 5:30 P.M., after which the parents may rough it or yield to staff "governesses"—a status way of saying babysitters. After visiting one such fount of family fun in Atlantic City, a travel writer was moved to rhapsodize:

"At a buffet dinner the children watch their favorite TV shows while they eat and then move into another TV room to continue watching their programs while the parents go to dinner in the regular dining rooms. . . ." And then, leaving this Shangri-la behind, he reported on the Big Picture in family vacationing: "Whether you let children participate in all trip activities or make use of the numerous special services available for their care and amusement . . . you will be free from the guilt or frustration you would feel if you left them home . . . or stayed home with them. There are many family resorts where special programs for children leave the parents free to enjoy their own recreation alone, if they wish, but where the family is together for enough hours in the day to enjoy the vacation as a unit. . . ."

"What it amounts to," says the manager of one such resort, "is conducting a camp under the scrutiny of the parents— and it's hell. It's very tough to pacify adults when it comes to children. The kid complains about something and mama comes right to the management. She always blames the management. Some boy says 'Fatty' to her fat little daughter, she blames the management. The parents don't want complaints. If the kids are unhappy it interrupts their *own* good time."

The gentleman sounds aggrieved, and this is understandable; if children are unhappy it is surely not the fault of the management, for never have managements worked more arduously to insure the contentment of the young. This particular holiday haven, located in upstate New York, provides for their pleasure: a supervised nursery; two splendidly equipped, fully staffed playrooms open seven hours day; bowling, ice skating, ping-pong, painting, arts and crafts, and group singing; swimming lessons and daily two-hour Splash Parties during which no adults are allowed into the pool; morning games for fun and prizes; afternoon games for fun and prizes; and, nightly, a children's carnival with wheels of fortune and other games of chance—nightly, that is, except for Movie Nights, Weiner Roast Nights, and Show Nights, the last featuring such hired professional entertainers as magicians and puppeteers.

With such a lineup, it is not surprising to find that the liveliest spot in the house is wherever the kiddies are. Parents find themselves somewhat in the same boat as the first-class voyager who notes from the silence of his splendid digs that all the action seems to be on the third-class deck. Like him, they may try to gate-crash—and they are spurned.

"We have to protect the kids' rights," says an assistant manager. "There'll be a party going on for the eight- to twelve-year-olds, you know, and the juke box is blasting and the kids are singing and yelling and dancing and having a ball. Pretty soon the grown-ups are crowding the doorway to see what's going on. We let them watch, but they can't go in. We're not nasty about it. We just say, 'Are *you* under twelve?' and usually they get embarrassed and go away." (During the winter vacation weeks in many resorts, children virtually take over. One manager recalls an evening when ten- to twelve-year-olds went from their scheduled after-dinner amusements to an impromptu dance session in a corner of the cocktail lounge, where a three-piece band played nightly for the adults' dancing pleasure. "At first everybody enjoyed watching them," he says, "but soon they were swarming all over the lounge. You couldn't move, you couldn't talk, the bartenders couldn't even hear the orders. The adults were demanding that we kick them out, but how do you do it? You get a kid by the back of the neck, you've got a lawsuit on your hands. The whole thing just went completely out of control." The manager took to the loudspeaker system, pleading with the tykes to clear out. In vain. It was finally necessary to dismiss the musicians, at which point the children dispersed and the cocktail lounge was turned back to its rightful occupants, sans music.)

In the big-city tourist hotels, services to children make up in elegance what they may lack in scope. Often the family group no sooner is installed in its quarters than a bellboy appears with a basket of fruit, compliments of the house. For the mother? Nonsense. For the children. Many hotels can't even wait that long but collar the child in the lobby and ply him with candy grab-bags and sightseeing kits while the parents are registering. In hotel dining rooms children get balloons, coloring books, and souvenir caps; parents get a respite, no gift horse to be looked in the mouth.

To lengthen that respite, city hotels lay in large stocks of baby-sitters. Some have supervised nurseries or play areas. Many have tie-in arrangements with what are called "children's tour services," an invention born not long ago out of pressing necessity. Such services will take the children sightseeing and, what with one tactic and another, keep them out of the parental path for as long as eight hours at a clip ("leaving you free," notes a brochure, "to shop . . . or catch that matinee. . . .").

One New York establishment recently summoned its think-ers to ponder what more could be done for the young, and came up with a courtesy-to-children campaign. Each child, upon being registered, was to be given a manila envelope which would contain a map of the city, notices of current entertainments and tours for children around and about town, free post cards, a Children's Menu for the day, coupons that might be exchanged for candy—and a letter of welcome direct from the manager. "Happy Holiday!" it read. "And while you and your parents are staying with us, we have a lot of fun things for you to enjoy. . . ." And concluded: "Go ahead, have a happy time, and bring your parents back again soon!"

This, of course, is the heart of the matter, and it delivers a two-way punch. "If the children are happy here, the parents will probably come back," says an official of the hotel. "But we are also insuring ourselves against the time when the children are grown. We are building pleasant associations. A grown-up will say, 'Oh, yes, I had a wonderful time at the Plaza when I was a child,' and he will return."

The Plaza falls within the vast domain of Mr. Conrad Hilton, a man who seems to love children as dearly as any-one in the business. In Chicago a Hilton Hotel has quiz shows and prizes for children; in Houston, gives awards to children who finish their milk; in Buffalo, dispenses free cookies to go with the milk. Other lights in the Hilton constellation have surprise satchels for children, supervised fun-and-games for children, Christmas and Easter parties for children, and hop-scotch rugs for children. But none shows the éclat of New York's Savoy Hilton, which maintains in its basement a bicycle and tricycle garage.

Even the great convention hotels, where in bygone years the patter of little feet was seldom heard, have learned that the early bird catches the child. The convention delegate is as loath as any other Good and Popular Parent to leave his young at home, and this has wrought a marked change in the character of conventions. Nowadays they are planned, as a hotel man points out, as vacations for the entire family; the number of children in attendance has doubled in five years and shows no sign of going anywhere but up.

Thus any convention hotel that wants to stay in the running has had to undergo drastic physical and psychological renovation. The first has prepared it to cater to children (convention hosts now stock heavy inventories of cribs, playpens, high chairs, disposable diapers, baby foods, baby powders, bottle warmers, and sterilized nipples); the second, to project an image of *wanting* to cater to children: one hotel is the proud employer, and so informs the public, of a room-service waiter who always tests a bottle of formula (cheerfully made up and heated by the kitchen staff) on his own wrist before he hands it over to mothers. *That's* image-building.

The convention hotels will match any bag of candy, basket of fruit, or sightseeing kit a child can get anywhere else. They also give conventioneering children swimming parties, bus tours, dinner banquets, and soda-pop cocktail parties; one provides a Children's Hospitality Room on the convention floor, *verboten* to adults and equipped with juke boxes, ping-pong tables, television sets, and, on wet days, movies. "Anything," says a management man, "to make the small fry happy."

With children thus whooping it up on the travel trails, the people who outfit them for travel are exceedingly busy and in understandably good spirits. "If it folds, it sells," says a buyer of children's travel accouterments. "But it's got to fold, or collapse, or do *something;* it can't just sit there. Takes up too much room.

"We are having a real boom in this merchandise. I haven't seen anything like it in twenty-two years. When I first went into the business there was very little of this stuff around; a baby's car seat here, a little travel crib there. But today—dozens and dozens of these travel items. More coming out all the time. With all these kids traveling, mothers will buy anything to make them comfortable. Saves wear and tear on the whole family."

Thus: collapsible playpens, portable cribs, convertible playpen-cribs, folding strollers, collapsible seats, folding car beds, pullmans that hook over car seats, travel toidies that fold into suit cases, screened-in collapsible cribs with telescopic legs—a multitude of fully portable gadgets and gewgaws by which the child himself, as Margaret Mead has noted in reviewing certain sociological aspects of the travel picture, "is made into a fully portable object."

These are primarily for the landlubber, but other comforts and conveniences await the child who goes by air or sea. The airlines, which are short on room aloft for play areas and such, resort to the ubiquitous special rate, which they offer with grace and enthusiasm. They have car beds for wee ones, and many small accommodations of the disposable-diaper variety. Hostesses, whose indoctrination has not neglected the child's place in travel today, will put off anything short of a midair collision to heat a baby's bottle, and when time permits they will make as much a fuss over children as any child or mother could desire.

Ships, having more time and more space, use them to prove to children that getting there is, indeed, half the fun. The ocean-going youngster has his play areas, his nurseries, his deck games, and his dining room—or at least his Special Sitting. He has planned activities by day and baby-sitters (the modern stewardess wears two hats) by night, and even when parents have to do their own sitting it is a relatively painless procedure. Having disembarked safely with a daughter too young to walk, one traveler wrote, in *My Baby* magazine, the following testimonial to Togetherness aboard ship: "While my husband went for a swim I took the baby to the lounge where she practiced creeping and attracted attention. Back to the cabin for a fresh disposable diaper, and then I took her to the gym to watch Daddy exercise. Next day he would take over while I took cha-cha lessons. . . . And so it went. The four days flew by. Seasickness? Yes. One morning half the passengers, including me, were laid low by a rough sea. The baby was, as are all babies, unaffected."

On many liners there are children-only hours in the ship's pool and gym. There are children's movies every morning, and supervised playrooms laden with toys are in operation eight hours a day (on a three-class ship there are, of course, three playrooms—"designed by child psychologists," one well-oriented line specifies, "and tastefully furnished with child-size furniture"). In these selfsame playrooms are held New Year's, Easter, Thanksgiving, and Christmas parties, the last replete with Santa Claus; not to speak of birthday parties, compliments of the house, whenever the occasions arise. And, at the appropriate time, governed by the appropriate protocol, a junior edition of the Captain's Dinner. "We treat children like V.I.P.'s," says a front-office salt. "After all, they are."

With so much to recommend them, the shipping lines lately have been enlightening parents on the economic advantages of ocean travel as opposed to, say, a motor tour. One company juggled some figures and came up with this delightful discovery, which it quickly communicated to parents via an extensive advertising campaign: A five-day voyage to Europe for a family of five—two large, three small—traveling off-season and third-class, costs no more than a five-day automobile trip in the native land, when one figures the price of food, motels, baby-sitters, and the like. "And when you get to Europe," says a company official, "you've got something to *see!*" (You've also, it follows, got something to *spend,* but why spoil a nice sales pitch?) Besides, as the man points out, foreign travel is broadening for children. "People say, 'I can't afford to take the family to Europe.' And then they take the wife and kids to Florida and spend a fortune, and when they're finished what have they seen? Nothing."

Unfortunately, the public school system fouls up this perfectly good line of reasoning. Most children just don't have time for an ocean junket to Europe in winter, when bargain rates prevail. But the winter cruise—ah, there is something else again. They have the time, they have the willing parents, and the travel people will supply the rest. Those Caribbean cruise lines whose Sunday punch once was the promise of shipboard romance have lately, like the convention hotels, changed their image. Now they push family package plans and special services for the young, and the glad cries of children merge with the native calypso beat. One cruise line even supplies tutors to keep the youngster on course, as he glides through the balmy waters, for his return to the harsh realities of school life.

And they *are* harsh realities. After the treatment Vacationland's most honored guest receives today, his return home must pose agonizing problems. And they will grow more agonizing yet, for the vacation folk apparently have only begun. "There is so much that *could* be done for children," says a resort public-relations man. "We've been very slow in setting up services for them. We are still very limited.

"You know, a really good program for children—a *really* good program—can work miracles. You get one satisfied child, you have two satisfied parents, you have three regular customers. You give me some moth-eaten resort and a decent budget and a year to set up the children's angle and promote it, and I'll fill the place to capacity. I've got some ideas. . . ."

Oh, child. Oh, wandering V.I.P. Take whatever they give and enjoy it, for tomorrow you will be all grown up and Vacationland, even if it has room for you, just will not be the same.

IN BUSINESS
Hit the Kids

Every advertiser's dream is a campaign aimed at kids that *works,*" says a Madison Avenue potentate. "I hear guys say you can't sell a kid anything he doesn't want. I don't believe it. With the right formula you can sell a kid *anything,* and you can depend on him to sell his parents. You gotta hit the kids. Hit the *kids,*" he repeats, thrusting a meaty fist toward an imaginary solar plexus.

Such is the fighting spirit that outraged observers have come to call "the insidious manipulation of children." The advertisers call it by kinder names, crying, as the old wheeze goes, all the way to the bank, to be so unjustly accused. Facts, they say, are facts. What the child wants the child probably will get. They are not manipulating him, they are merely serving him; and if in the execution of such good works they gather some shekels, is this not after all the American Way?

Indeed so. Child worship is the almighty dollar's true friend. "The future occupation of all moppets is to be skilled consumers," sociologist David Riesman has written. The future is upon us: by the grace of his Good Parent and the sweat of the adman, today's moppet is already a highly skilled consumer who, even when he doesn't make the purchase himself, knows full well where to send Mommy and what to tell her to buy.

Nor is his influence restricted to the realm of children's products. Encouraged by the fact that the child virtually dictates the purchase of breakfast foods and cereals, advertisers some time back happened upon the notion that he might make an effective ally in matters of toothpastes and dishwashers as well. They did a great deal of very expensive research which, of course, proved them right; and today it is widely held along Madison Avenue that if you can hook a child you hook his parent, *ipso facto* and Q.E.D.

Thus, while everybody loves a young'un, nobody loves him like the advertisers, who chase him with passion and court him with lust. They spend millions yearly to depth-study their way into his heart, they sic psychologists and motivational researchers onto his psyche, they form panels, attend conferences, sit in grave council to determine what color packaging, what premium, what jingle, what formula will wring from the mouths of babes those five magic words, "Mom, buy *that* for me," that fill the adman's heart with joy and gladness.

Reams have been written about the purchasing power of teen-agers, who comprise 10 per cent of the consumer market. But children under teen-age make up almost 30 per cent of the market, a sun-ripened plum indeed. There are around fifty million of them in the nation, and their numbers grow torrentially, five million more being expected by 1965. What was before the advent of TV a pliable but hard-to-hit market is now a wondrously accessible, collective sitting duck, just waiting to be picked off by the advertiser who knows his small game.

It is hardly respectable anymore for an advertiser to launch a campaign aimed at children without first hiring some research outfit to plumb their depths. Such studies may, and often do, yield findings of limited urgency ("Why pay a guy $10,000 for a lot of Freudian double-talk on why kids like red, when we know to begin with that kids like red?" says one agency man), but clients still consider them the fashionable approach to marketing. So the researchers are forever sounding out vast numbers of children on such issues as: Do you like to see baseball gloves named after ball players? (Yes—57.5 per cent); At equal prices, would you prefer an American or an imported bicycle? (59.9 per cent are loyal to the home team); and, clearly the most vital of all, Do you get an allowance? (64.1 per cent of the nation's kiddies do, according to one survey). Many advertising agencies, in addition, have their own large panels of youngsters on call via the mails; and magazines that carry advertising for children's products, or products whose purchase children may influence, do their own surveys.

Nothing is sacred; even the Boy Scouts are enlisted in the aid of Madison Avenue's grandest ventures. The research staff of *Boys' Life,* the Boy Scout magazine, from time to time surveys its readers for "the latest basic market data on all phases of boy activity," and from the masses of material thus culled offers advertisers such tidbits as these: most Boy Scouts who use chapped-lip medications use them in winter, 68.3 per cent pick out their own shoes, and 34 per cent have at some time used advertised products to cure poison ivy (here, the commercial prognosis is good: more of those Boy Scout camping trips should send sales zooming).

On behalf of a client who had launched three new dolls and wanted to test the effect of his advertising, one agency hired a psychologist to "do a literature search—that is, read everything and find out whatever had been done that would tell us about little girls. It was hoped that through this study we would gain insight into the motivations of little girls vis-à-vis dolls." The psychologist duly read and read but came up with little that told the agency people anything about little girls vis-à-vis dolls they hadn't known in the first place. So they switched their methodology (a favored word when seeking ways to hook children; it lends a modest scientific air to what otherwise might seem unconscionable). They got together groups of little girls and watched them, under control conditions, playing with the dolls.

This wasn't too successful either, it developed. The agency then sent out researchers to interview two hundred little girls individually in their homes. Their finding was that while doll X, heretofore the most heavily advertised of the three and in fact the sales leader, was the girls' favorite when seen on TV, it was only the *second* favorite when they were given the dolls to play with. Thus proving just what the agencies love to have such studies prove: that advertising is what makes the sun shine bright.

And nowhere is this truer than in the realm of children's products. "For God's sake," says an adman with a private aversion to the whole business, "let's *hope* that the quality of the product plays some part in adult brand preference. But the kids, you see, are so impressionable, so malleable, that they will want anything you tell them they *should* want, if you tell them often enough and in the right way.

"A kid isn't as concerned as his parents with raising his own status in the group; he is concerned merely with *belonging* to the group. Speak to him lovingly and approvingly, make him feel that *he will belong* if he only gets thus and such, and he won't leave his parents alone until he gets it."

The two peerless examples are in the toy and cereal fields. Toy makers now have their salesmanship down to such a finely honed science that sales people and executives interviewed in a dozen large toy and department stores well before Christmas predicted with almost total accuracy what the ten top sellers would be. "You don't have to ask me what will sell," one said, "all you have to do is see what's advertised on TV." What was on TV, that season, were several monster robot-type toys, one of which was so monumentally unattractive that very small children burst into tears when they saw it on the home screen. These sold as if they were being given away. ("I felt like putting an ad in the paper reading, 'Yes, we have all the TV monsters, but why don't you buy your child a *toy?*'" said one store buyer.) Other big television items were a talking doll with a repertoire of some ten lines including "Let's have a picnic," "Let's have a party," and "I *love* you," and a wind-up doll that filled home screens across the nation with most distressing writhings and wigglings, rather like an infant with dreadful gas pains. All of these were eminently successful.

"I can remember when this business was fun," said an executive at Macy's, where—as everywhere else—the heavily advertised toys were given priority display spots. "But nowadays it's all TV manipulation. I don't like to see the kiddies being victimized by TV sponsors. [An astonishing point of view, one may note; if Mommy is harangued into going right out for the toy that's only $19.95, has kiddie indeed been victimized? Oh, Mr. Macy!] It's gotten so bad that, when we place our orders, we're no longer shown the toy, we're shown the commercial. One manufacturer has this Mystery Item. Nobody even knows what it is. But there are jobbers who have already bought it by the bushel on the strength of a $4,500,000 TV budget. Is this Toyland?"

Against such uncharitable attacks, the toy men and the agency people stand united. "The big TV toys sell because they are *good* toys," says an adman. "If they weren't, the kids wouldn't buy them. Furthermore, you can't blame the medium if parents indulge their children. If the parent doesn't want to buy the thing he ought to be able to say No. Why the hell should he put the burden of blame on us? I'm tired of playing the heavy; any parent who is in command at home has no quarrel with us."

This is a noble dodge, but a dodge nonetheless. When aiming at the child consumer, advertisers have no greater purpose than to hoist by his own petard the parent who can still say No. "Whereas," begins one extensive report to a national toy company, "parents of past generations relied upon discipline and common sense, today's parents do not fully trust their judgment and intuition . . . [and, the echo trails, a good thing, too]. They appear equally afraid to both deny and to indulge their children. As the child grows old enough to 'sense' the parental indecision, he soon learns to manipulate it to his ends, exerting pressure toward the purchase of specific toys."

Regarding such pressure, the report suggested that the client might provide some folklore or historic background which the child could use to "justify" the purchase to his parents. For example, citing the positive appeal of a toy rocket fired by water and thus, understandably, no favorite with parents: "Promotion . . . directed at parents should exploit the following motivating themes: (a) Rockets are educational—they teach boys important scientific principles. (b) Your little boy may be a future space traveler or scientist. You should encourage his interest. (c) Rockets are the thing of the future. Everybody should learn about them. (d) Rockets are shared fun for the whole family."

It is largely from this school of thinking that the industry's big push for the "educational" plaything has evolved. The "educational" label, it is felt, is a great parental guilt-reliever, and does nothing to dampen the child's enthusiasm so long as the toy is not too educational. Thus many toy makers and agencies have enlisted education experts to "age-grade" and "educator-approve" playthings that used to be simply fun. A sexy doll, as was noted earlier, may be considered educational because she teaches tots a thing or two about high fashion; a gun may be plugged as educational because it "brings our heritage alive," and a transistor radio because the child who owns one will hear the news broadcasts (all these approaches have been market-tested by agencies, with exemplary success).

If the "educational" pitch does not suffice, the researchers have other suggestions to offer. In a trade magazine called *Motivations,* toy makers are advised the following subliminal suggestions to adults may sell a toy or two:

"1. Toys are lessons in emotional partnership. Modern society, especially in the city, offers little opportunity for parents and children to engage in meaningful, purposeful activity together. . . . Toys help to overcome this gap. . . . 2. Toys mean love. . . . 3. Toys allow parents to 'regress' in an acceptable way."

And now to the gut of the matter: "Toys are a means of 'making up' for [parental] failure. Show the unadulterated joy of the child and how the toy he has received draws him close to his parents."

Such outré emotional capers are happily not always called for. For the run-of-the-mill parent who feels at least reasonably well loved, the toy industry holds that the "educational" sales gimmick is appealing enough to turn the trick. In this the industry hews close to the predominant national view that there is no education like a science education; and thus, it clearly follows, there is no educational toy like a science-educational toy. The agencies recently have taken to describing almost anything that is battery-operated—and today astounding numbers of toys are—as scientific. "Scientific," they find, is a handy label to pin on military toys, which parents traditionally find objectionable but buy anyway.

"I try to create as many non-military items as possible," says Chicagoan Marvin Glass, a toy designer who has turned out some top sellers, notably robots, of recent seasons, "but children themselves want toys with combat. Kids expect their toys to reflect the complexity of the real world. We live, after all, in a social structure in which power is a big factor, and you can't segregate toys from that structure. Instead of looking at the idyllic concept of childhood as a perfectly happy time, I look at the child as a frustrated Lilliputian, forced into subservience in an adult world. I try to compensate for that by creating toys that give him a sense of being the boss." A gainful aim.

Mr. Glass's most successful toys have been backed by immense advertising budgets for television, whose effectiveness perhaps is best illustrated by the case of the Yo-Yo, a humble plaything with a long and generally honorable history. First produced in this country in the early 1920's, a rage in the '40's, and an unobtrusive staple ever since, the Yo-Yo had remained in business largely through the herculean efforts of Yo-Yo demonstraters, who plied their trade in schools across the nation. Several seasons ago the Yo-Yo chieftains decided to try television advertising for the first time. They embarked upon a vast regional promotion, filling the TV screen with Yo-Yo men manipulating the bauble downward, upward, sideways, and through a colossal gamut of tricky maneuvers most observers had never known could be coaxed out of a Yo-Yo. Now, the Yo-Yo is not scientific, it is not automatic, and not even its makers would claim that it is educational. But in the season after its television debut it sold ten million units, more than the combined sales volume of all the preceding years.

The industry's standard-bearers for the Educational Toy can hardly begrudge the Yo-Yo its brilliant comeback, although several diehards among them have suggested that the main reason it enjoyed such success was because it *is,* in fact, educational.

The toys the industry loves best, however, are those that not only broaden the child's horizons but teach mommy a thing or two as well. Among many cases in point are the kitchen-center gadgets for little girls which have toy refrigerators amply stocked with such items as Kellogg's Corn Flakes and Gerber Baby Foods; this is the kind of promotional tie-in that catches a girl-child coming and going, and gives a fine prod to the associative processes of her mother. Similarly, pint-sized cooking and baking sets come equipped with miniature packages of brand-name mixes. "The kids usually want those little packages replaced by the same brand," an adman says happily. "And if the *kid's* cake has come out well, we may make a regular customer of the mother, too."

In this merging of interests between the toy and food folk, the toy people have much to gain. For the food men (in particular, the candy and cold-cereal men) are, by Madison Avenue consensus, absolute geniuses in the delicate art of h_zoking a child and, it follows, his parents. "In the old days," says a spokesman for one of the breakfast-food giants, "kids ate what their mothers put in front of them. Seems strange, doesn't it? Now there is no question who is boss. The kids tell their mothers what to buy. We can make customers out of them before they can read. We love kids. So do the supermarket people. ["Love kids?" said a supermarket man when queried on this very point. "Well, we do every last thing we can to attract them. But if it weren't for the fact that they hold the reins on the money, we wouldn't let the little monsters past the front door."] Sure, we're using children. So what? It's not like we're selling them poison. This stuff is *good* for them."

With its conscience thus clear, the industry has been applying the leverage to its market—primarily, six- to twelve-year-olds—so successfully that sales of ready-to-eat cereals have risen to a stratospheric $440 million a year, almost five times the retail sales figures before the advent of television. The magic has been wrought by the use of several wondrous formulas (sample, from a top advertising agency's rule book: "Appeal to the herd instinct; a kid wants everything, but the thing he *really* wants is something other kids have."—"Love them; kids are just as neurotic as the rest of us."—"Involve them; kids are all ego monsters, they want to get in on the act."—"Don't command them; kids nowadays won't take it from their parents, why the hell should they take it from us?") which have enabled the industry to pummel the nation's toddlers into a sweet pulp of accommodation.

Despite all the research, however, nobody has as yet come up with anything better than the premium gimmick, grandaddy of all those devices that put child worshipers right where the kings of commerce want them. The production of child-appeal premiums is a highly specialized business today.

There are, generally, two varieties: the giveaway or "insert," which goes directly into the cereal box, and what is called the "self-liquidating" variety, which is mailed to the customer upon receipt of small change and box tops. By the time a child has done a week's TV-watching stint, he has committed to memory every detail of the premiums currently available and is fully prepped to take over for the cereal people and further their cause within the home.

Breakfast-food admen with small children do not have to step beyond their own front doors to discover whether their current campaigns are hitting the target. "My five-year-old watches a commercial one night," says one, "and if it doesn't smack him in the face he sees the same commercial the next night, and the M.C. tells him, 'If you haven't told Mommy to buy this yet, tell her NOW.' And my kid runs into the kitchen and yells, 'Mommy, buy it NOW!' Or if he keeps his mouth shut at home, as soon as my wife sets him loose in the supermarket he starts running around until he finds the right package. When he begins needling her to buy my client's product I know we're on the right track; otherwise, I know something is wrong with our sales pitch."

Sam Gold and Associates, one of the top premium producers, addresses prospective clients as follows: "By tying these proven sales stimulants in with your product . . . you can get millions of little kings across the country to say: 'Mom, please get that for me!' . . . Let us show you how you, too, can *cash in on kids!*"

Since, as one study shows, nearly 80 per cent of children ask their parents to buy certain brands, and since, moreover, 73.6 of the parents comply, the premium folk obviously are speaking from a highly defensible posture. "We believe," one of them says, "that American children are the world's greatest sales force. The American mother wants her kid to be happy, no matter what. She may complain about the way he makes her buy the box and doesn't eat the cereal, but *she buys it.* Anyway, the kid is getting a better deal than she does. What does she get with a bar of soap that's supposed to give her a radiant, lovely complexion? Tell me *that* when you talk about 'insidious manipulation of kids.' At least we give him a toy that has"—waving an arm expansively toward the shelves laden with miniscule missiles and secret-compartment pirate rings—*"educational* value."

The power of premiums does not, of course, stop with children's food products. They have been used to sell youngsters cheese, meats, teas and tuna fish, soaps and shampoos, pharmaceuticals and shoes, and even beer, as well as to pressure children to point their parents' noses toward the right automobiles, radios, television sets, refrigerators, home freezers and other appliances, and even banks and department stores. Typically, a prize is offered to the child who shows up at the retail dealer's with parent in tow. The child finds the premium hard to resist and the parent, naturally, finds the child impossible to resist, and thus do the wheels of commerce turn.

The right kind of packaging can rack up heavy mileage with children, too. Trade publications in the packaging field regularly publish articles with such titles as "Get 'Em Young," and motivational research reports have yielded up the suggestions that package copy should be straight, urgent, and monosyllabic, that trademarks should tie in with TV characters, and that children are hooked fastest and best by multi-purpose packages, such as those that may be converted into airplanes or gasoline stations. ("Does the package almost ask the child to slyly drop it in the shopping cart?" asks Eugene Gilbert of Gilbert Youth Research, which keeps an unblinking eye on that juicy target known as the "youth market.")

A corn flake is, after all, just a corn flake, but the packages are marvels of technology. Product boxes have boasted playable phonograph records, panels that may be cut up into mock villages with dozens of moving parts, Disneyland scenes that can be illuminated by inserting a bulb through the front of the package. For children old enough to read, the wrappers speak bluntly: "The easiest candies to get mother to buy— they're pure wholesome Kraft foods—that's why!"

Manufacturers of products for all-family use come in through the back door—it is wide open—to grab the kiddies and set them up for all their tomorrows. A typical maneuver: Advertisement pictures little girl and little boy small-talking at a party. Copy reads: "You'll be using makeup soon, that's why you should use Dial Soap now!" ("I got paid for my professional sins," says a copywriter, "when my daughter came to me, terribly worried, and said, 'Mother, if we don't buy *I*pana, how will I be a deb*u*tante when I grow up?' I thought, 'Dammit, *must* they fill my child's head with such drivel?'— and then the irritation passed, and all I could think was that it really wasn't a bad copy line.")

Even when the message is not directed to the child, advertisers can depend on him to hear and to spread the word. "He sits there, in front of the TV set," says an adman. "His mind is untrammeled, he doesn't have a thousand other concerns like adults do, and so he is infinitely more receptive to our message. Very often he is the first to know of new products. He acts as a sort of information bureau in the house. When the family talks about a new refrigerator he is the one who says, 'We should get *that kind* with the movable shelf.' Or when it's a new car, and the parents are undecided, the one small voice that says, '*I* want us to get so-and-so' can make the sale. The parents see no big difference between all the competing claims, so they figure they may as well make the

kid happy. The influence children have in this way is incalculable." There are, further, the contest hooks: "Bring
Mom to your nearest washing-machine dealer and get an
entry blank"—and the tots deliver. In one big national promotion they delivered better than a million parents to service
stations across the country carrying a certain brand of oil;
on the regional level they have delivered thousands of parents to supermarkets to make the initial purchase that would
permit them to enter the contest, and to department stores,
where kiddies were awarded prizes for parents spending the
most money. One entrepreneur, in a virtuoso display of how
to cash in on kids, even ran an ad-writing contest for children.
Required for entry: one box top. "If American parents didn't
try so hard to please their kids," says an agency man forthrightly, "we wouldn't be able to coast two yards on these
promotions."

Thus the manipulators are vindicated. They have even
managed—and it can't have been too easy—to hammer out
a near-charitable Ethic of their own, which renders them not
only innocent but *pro bono publico*.

"The environment of the modern child," writes one of the
positive thinkers in the consumer-motivation field, "is charac-
terized by ceaseless change which at the same time that it
fascinates the child also threatens him. The rituals of ad slo-
gans, of singing commercials, of endless repetitions of the
same ad in a saturation campaign become, in this context of
change, fixed points of reference, elements of stability in an
ever-changing environment.

"And when the child goes with his parents on shopping
expeditions, which are again explorations into the unknown,
memories of the encounters with advertising become like a
map guiding the child, giving him the security of seeing something familiar and known. . . ."

Thus it becomes clear that when children are involved, no facet of commerce is too mundane to be Psychologically Significant. The food and toy men make the point, but to find it made with true panache, one must turn to the diaper-service industry, a fifty-million-dollar-a-year métier which the world has taken lightly long enough.

This band of commercial pioneers has come a far, far way from manifestly humble origins, and has displayed en route a stunning awareness of the prevailing parental mood. Note the historical predicament of the diaper-service men. The food man sold an animal cracker, which was good to eat. The toy man sold a doll, which was fun to play with. But the diaper man? Faced with his own dismal image, he took action. He stopped selling diaper service and started selling superiority: better care for better babies. Ergo: Diaper service, traditionally a laundry, became a profession, and possibly even a calling. Today it is a public utility, a corporate uncle, a family counselor second in good works only to the pediatrician himself. This is a lot of image to distill from a rented dydee, and the diaper people admittedly had help. Much of what they are and more of what they seem to be, they owe to motivational research.

Several seasons back, seeking ways to extend their coverage, the diaper men consulted with a depth-study group. The diaper people wanted to know if their sales approach was right, if their image was good, if they were loved. Find out, they enjoined the researchers, how people *really* feel about diapers.

These injunctions resulted in a great many depth interviews with a great many parents and, eventually, a report that probes deeper and pokes harder into the parental psyche than possibly any other study ever done in behalf of a children's product. The report is a book-length dissertation upon the psychodynamics of the diaper, a product with so many emotional, psychological, and sociological—not to speak of physiological—ramifications that one feels a chowderhead not to have realized it all in the first place.

The scope is indicated by the table of contents, which serves up, among other choice bits:

> The Psychological Climate of Diaper Service
> The Dynamics of Diaper Service Psychology
> Creating a New Image of Diaper Service

Its awesomely analytic tone is established at the outset:

"Our main finding is that the diaper, and therefore Diaper Service, is not a matter-of-fact aspect of infant hygiene, but is a highly colored emotional product. . . . The attitudes toward Diaper Service are colored by and automatically grow out of the highly charged emotional climate surrounding the mother's feelings about the birth and care of her baby. . . . This is especially true of her feelings about diapers which are so peculiarly personal to the baby, and in psychological terms almost a part of, an extension of, the infant. . . . Since . . . Diaper Service cannot be presented simply as a utilitarian service, it is most important to understand these emotional and psychological factors which will make it possible for the Diaper Service Industry to be presented in a new image, ready and capable of fulfilling a new role."

Interpreting the psychological climate first, the researchers present their findings on the motivations of users and non-users of diaper service. The users were by and large cordial when depth-studied as to their attitudes on motherhood, babies, diapers, diaper-service delivery men, and the like. Asked to describe her feelings toward the delivery truck driver, one replied: "He's very friendly, very nice to know. . . . He's always asked me who's pregnant so he can drum up their business, and we always joke about it—I usually say, 'You mean who's pregnant besides me, because I'm practically always pregnant.' " Other interviewees reported similarly warm relationships with the diaper-service man. Only one was downright petty and uncooperative, replying, when asked about *her* truck driver, "I didn't look deep into his heart and soul, because it was not important to me."

The non-users, on the other hand, were a generally hostile group. They made unkind comments about the diaper-service mother, such as: "She's lazy." "She's extravagant." "She can't love her baby very much if she won't even wash his diapers." And: "No GOOD mother ever uses diaper service." Thus it was clear to the researchers that the wash-your-own woman views diaper service as an admission of inadequacy, self-indulgence, and baby rejection. She feels guilty—on an unconscious level, of course—about her worth as a mother, "and she frequently works out her guilt by a compulsive need to do the diapers herself.

"Before the mother is able to be sold sterile diapers," they continue, "the Diaper Service Industry may have to sell the mother the conviction that she can be a BETTER MOTHER because she will have more love and more time for baby if she doesn't enslave herself to diaper washing. . . .

"It seems clear from these findings that the first job that faces the Diaper Service Industry is an educational project which will in effect give the mother *moral permission* [italics the author's] to have Diaper Service; provide absolution for what she may have considered laziness."

Yes, but how? To get the methodology across to the diaper-service people, who perhaps had never realized the pertinancy of such concepts to the laundry business, the researchers borrow a metaphor from chemistry: "The mother needs to develop rationalizations which help her resolve her conflicts. . . . Each rationalization that she develops represents a point of crystallization in which Diaper Service appears as a resolution of her unconscious problems. Chemists speak of a 'supersaturated solution,' a solution already so overloaded that the addition of a single crystal more will cause everything suspended in solution to crystallize and fall to the bottom. The mother's feelings are like this solution. She is held 'in suspension.' She wants Diaper Service. She has conflicts about it. So she does nothing. *But* each rationalization that she can develop brings her closer and closer to the point of finally 'crystallizing' a decision. . . .

"We have found that the rationalizations which can serve as points of crystallization are of three major kinds:

"1. Clinical: Diaper Service helps to reinforce the mother's image of herself as the INFANT'S PROTECTOR.

"2. Emotional: Diaper Service helps the mother have CONFIDENCE in herself as a WIFE AND MOTHER.

"3. Social: Diaper Service is the MODERN SOLUTION; it is ACCEPTABLE and even DESIRABLE in TODAY'S SCHEME of things."

This last is a tricky factor since, as with so many status considerations, what is *de rigueur* in one neighborhood may be unforgivably gauche in another. One mother, recently moved from a housing development to a fine residential pocket just outside Boston, says: "Around here you not only have to take diaper service, you have to keep it for a couple of years. It's a prestige thing, like hiring a live-in nurse for three weeks when you bring the baby home from the hospital. But in the old neighborhood nobody had diaper service. It was considered very bad form, like not getting up to make your husband breakfast. I felt so ashamed to be different that I told the routeman to pull his truck way up into the driveway, so the neighbors wouldn't see it." (A common ruse, according to diaper-service men. "When you're in this business," one says, "you really know we're living in a class society.")

For those who aren't won over by status appeals, the depth-study people advise wooing with Image. Diaper service, they suggest, should be a kindly counselor: "In this role the Diaper Service company should seek to find a place next to the pediatrician's in importance to the mother of a first baby; and with more experienced mothers even to replace the pediatrician in areas such as baby's external physical care and hygiene." (For which the pediatrician, it may be noted, could hardly be more grateful.) "Humanize and personalize Diaper Service. . . . Never forget that you are dealing with a mother's feelings toward her baby and not with a rational product. Appeal to her feelings."

Appeal as well, the depth fellows stress, to the father's feelings. "In our society father frequently plays the role of auxiliary mother. . . . Father changes baby's diapers, washes baby's diapers, feeds baby, dresses, airs baby. . . . The father's tendency therefore is to seek the easiest possible way to do these jobs. . . . Diaper Service answers this convenience factor." And then: "Diaper Service should make the husband feel important." (Even the man who won't do diapers, the report cannily notes, can be made to feel important: "Diaper Service is the husband's opportunity to be the gracious giver.")

With new psychological insight and a new image, the diaper men were almost set to go. There remained only the problem of, as the trade puts it, "extending the customer life of the Diaper Service user." Now, in the diaper business, this clearly is a delicate problem. It is possible to extend the customer life of, say, a baby-oil user by creating new uses for baby oil; but the customer life of a diaper-service user can be extended only—one must face the problem squarely—by going powerful slow on toilet training.

Here the researchers tread softly. The evidence suggests, they say, that when the child is about six months old there comes a time of reckoning, wherein the mother begins to think serious thoughts about discontinuing the service. Therefore, a subtle promotional campaign to change her thinking may be indicated. "The Diaper Service Industry should be careful to avoid the appearance of applying pressure, but should rather seek to subtly employ the emotional and psychological appeals which would be most effective in convincing the mother to continue."

What emotional and psychological appeals? "Well," said a diaper man recently, "we tell our mothers how early toilet training accounts for neurotics. I mean, that's no *lie!* It *does,* absolutely! Besides, that's the kind of talk they like to hear."

Now the specter of our future citizens marching into kindergarten and even beyond, still wrapped in the tender ministrations of the diaper-service industry, would be nothing to worry about if the diaper-laundering community had said pshaw and gone about its scrubbing. But while some derisive snorts surely must have been heard, the industry at large set about building a new image and absolving wash-it-yourself mothers of guilt. Their efforts were well rewarded. To the surprise of no one in the research ranks, the remarkable thing about their baroque approach to dydees is that it works. Hark to a diaper-service man, overlord of a middling-sized metropolitan operation:

"I made up a presentation that tells our salespeople how to use those three basic rationalizations: the clinical, the emotional, and the social. It's very effective. We used to have a big problem with stolen diapers. Research showed us that many mothers felt guilty about taking diaper service, which made them resent us. So they were unconsciously punishing us by stealing our diapers. But since we started helping them get rid of their guilt feelings, we don't get that problem much any more."

From another precinct: "You can always tell which mothers feel guilty about using the diaper service. They call every day to complain about something—the diapers came late, or they weren't fluffy enough, or they were one diaper short. The truth is that this kind of woman doesn't really want diaper service at all, but she can't cancel it because it was a gift from the in-laws, or something like that. It's the kind of mother who says, 'Anything that goes on my baby I've got to take care of myself.'

"Well, what do you do with mothers like that? We used to lose them early. But now, when we run into a mother who feels she mustn't relinquish her God-given right to wash her kid's diapers, we help her rationalize. We show her how diaper service makes her a better mother. When our telephone saleswomen talk to a new prospect, they say, 'Diaper service will give you more time to love your baby.' If she says she already *has* enough time to love her baby, they say 'Certainly you want to give your baby the best of everything, and the best diapers are those which have been scientifically processed.' If she says she can do a real good job at home, they say, 'When you became pregnant you didn't go to just any medical man, did you? You went to a professional obstetrician. When you want your baby's diapers washed, you should go to a professional diaper service.' That pitch is usually effective."

Heartened by evidences that the psychodynamic approach is a solid one, the industry continues to delve deeper into the subliminal consumer. The Diaper Service Industry Association, an official spokesman, has carried on the pioneering work of the researchers with subsequent studies of the Reluctant Mother, and has made its findings available to members. (One such undertaking, called "The Quit Study," parsed to exhaustion the profoundest motivations of women who quit taking diaper service within six weeks, which is, in the industry's view, an inexcusably short time, and incidentally turned up an informative nugget about child-centeredness in the better-heeled classes. The early quitter, called "Mrs. Short-Short" by the research team, is typically in a low-income, low-education group, has lots of children born close together, and discontinues diaper service as soon as she can make it back to the scrubbing board. Mrs. Long-Long, a college type with more money and fewer children, will keep renting diapers as long as nature demands. She talks a great deal about how those scientifically processed dydees are better for her baby's health, and how they give her more free time to spend with the wee one and all the family. But she is a phony, this Long-Long. "She *hides* behind the health factor," say the researchers, not at all disapprovingly. "Our study shows that the mothers most likely to claim that they want to spend more time with baby, actually spend the most time *away from home and baby*." Design for action: You'll never make a Short-Short into a Long-Long, but at least try to help her rationalize her way into being an In-Between; as for the Long-Long, just let her do what comes naturally.)

"The people who have made a lot of money in this business are the ones who take advantage of our studies," says a man from the Diaper Service Industry Association. "They have built an image. They fill a real need in our society. Mothers can rely on them." Or, as an association brochure puts it: "Diaper service is a guardian of the health of baby America."

Bearing this considerable responsibility upon their avuncular shoulders, the diaper men today dispense all manner of good works. They sponsor an educational program in more than 2,500 high schools throughout the country, teaching students How to Be a Better Baby Sitter; it takes an exceptionally slow student (and future mother) not to understand by the time the program is done that diaper service is better for baby. The diaper companies also distribute baby-care magazines, hold "maternity teas" to give prospective mothers tips on how to fasten a faster diaper, and hire "baby-care counselors" to whom mothers may apply for information and advice. One Australian firm—the Diaper Service Industry Association's interest is global—has a retired chief of nursing who visits new mothers in the hospital to counsel, congratulate, and make the pitch for diaper service; but, the Association notes regretfully, "the A.M.A. frowns on our doing that here."

Nonetheless, much can be done within the unhappily rigorous limits set by the A.M.A. "We use all women in our sales force," says a local diaper man. "A mother will talk more freely to another woman. One of our saleswomen calls up, and the mother can tell her how it was in the labor room and all that. It makes a kind of a rapport, and once you establish that you have the client."

Here arises a key question in the industry: How do the saleswomen know whom to call? Locating potential clients early is so crucial, and the diaper-service people do such a masterly job of ferreting, that expectant mothers often hear from the diaper man almost as soon as they themselves know the good news, and sometimes before. "I was approached by three diaper-service firms when I was only five weeks pregnant," one typically reports. "Besides my husband and me, the only people who knew were my doctor and my best friend. How in the world did they get my name?"

Elementary.

"You watch the birth announcements and phone girls who

have just had babies," says a diaper-service man, opening his own bag of tricks. "You tell them, 'If you give us the names of your friends who are expecting we will send you a baby magazine.' Or a baby thermometer or a baby spoon. Anything that's easy to mail, you see. Then you call *those* names and make the same pitch. You can build up quite a nice mailing list that way.

"Or you pay a department store to let you set up a little display with a goldfish bowl. A shopper drops her pregnant friends' names into the bowl and she gets a free gift, maybe a couple of baby hangers.

"Or you tell your customers you are running a contest for your routemen, and the driver who turns in the most names of pregnant women will win a valuable prize, so won't they please cooperate for the sake of the driver, who sure could use that prize? That's a very successful gimmick.

"Of course, we don't just rely on friends," he says, with conspiratorial good nature. "There are all kinds of people who are in a good position to know who is pregnant very early in the game, and they don't mind making some extra cash for the information. Take druggists. They know the story as soon as a woman starts bringing in certain prescriptions from an obstetrician. People in the testing labs. The clerk who books maternity reservations in the hospital—she gives you the reservations list and you give her a gift, say a hundred dollars a month. There are even doctors who will go along, and if you can't get to the obstetrician maybe you can get to his nurse.

"Sometimes you make a deal with a maternity shop or a baby-furniture store. They give you their names and you give them your names. If you have the time and patience, you can just open a telephone book and go down the line. A lot of diaper-service operators do it. You tell the party you work for the city—you don't say *which* city—and do they know anyone who is pregnant because you're doing a survey for a new school or a new hospital and you need to project the population figures. If they start asking questions you just hang up. I won't say all these methods are completely on the level, but what harm are you doing?"

If several companies, in one way or another, should light upon the same woman's name, her choice may depend upon the bonus offer. A good bonus must have status value, such as gold-plated diaper pins, or be genuinely desirable, such as free baby pictures. Many companies use the picture gambit, and some even offer a free baby picture yearly for the first five years, which makes the company look magnanimous and gives the photography studio a ready-made foot in the door.

There is a minority of diaper-service operators, brave and lonely souls, who shun the bonus approach. "Gimmicks, just cheap gimmicks," says one. "Some people will go to any extreme to get a customer. They offer a gift and lower their standard of service. What do we care about gifts? We care about *babies*. What good is a premium if some helpless baby gets a diaper rash from an inferior diaper, eh? Diaper rash is untold suffering. Our mothers don't want some silly premium, they want *the best for their babies*."

Among mothers who go after the very best, no bonus the diaper services hand out is as successful as that *ne plus ultra* of the dydee world, the monogrammed diaper: a great gimmick, a great innovation and, as sage men say of so many great innovations, simplicity itself.

"We never solicit business," says the justly prideful owner of a thriving personalized diaper service. "We have three thousand customers, and they have all come to us by recommendation. One mother sees her friend's baby wearing monogrammed diapers, and she wants them for her baby, too. It's very natural.

"Our mothers order the initials when they are in the hospital. The monograms are in red, which is easiest to spot on a white background. We get many requests for three initials, but we never deviate from our policy. Just two are used. We use numbers as well as initials, so we have a double check. If the baby's initials are J.K., for instance [an association surely forgivable in this rarefied sphere], his diapers would also have the number 541-A. There can be no error. The baby *must get his own diapers back every time.*

"I will admit, it is a purely psychological appeal. Hygienically we don't need individualized diapers. But so many mothers are panicky about their babies, you see. The mother can become quite hysterical thinking her child is using a diaper another infant has used. Even my own wife—she knows as well as I do that a sterilized diaper is a sterilized diaper. But she feels happier and healthier using the personalized service. Wouldn't any mother?"

Not necessarily. The issue of what kind of diaper service is best for baby is one that some mothers ponder at length, and from their ponderings have emerged two distinct philosophies. The first holds that there is no diaper like a personal diaper. The second vigorously supports anonymous diapers.

"We were discussing this at bridge one day," a mother recently commented, without the slightest trace of self-consciousness, "and a lot of the girls said individual service isn't as good, because the personal diapers are washed in nets and there isn't a free flow in the washing machine. When everybody's diapers are done together there are no nets and they all get tossed around like mad, which really gives them a *good* wash.

"Actually, I prefer doing the diapers myself. I have a special system that is as good as any diaper service." For the edification of other insurgents, here it is: "First I rinse the diapers

in cold water. Then I fill the machine with boiling hot water
and put in a germ killer and two detergents. Why two? I don't
know. It *feels* cleaner. Then I reset the machine for cold and
put in a water softener. My friends think I'm a compulsive nut,
but I pride myself that none of my children has ever gotten
diaper rash."

A last question, then: Do or do not diapers all come out
the same in the wash? The answer comes from a diaper-service
public relations man, one of a vastly talented breed:

"Oh, Lord. We don't wash diapers. Mothers *wash* diapers.
We *process* them."

And what does process mean?

"Process means wash. But we wouldn't want to call it that.
We are a service, not a laundry. Psychologically speaking, we
are on the ball."

None will deny it. In the current climate, most any mole-
hill can grow up to be a mountain if it has to do with children.
Toy manufacturers know the trick. Dry-cereal makers know
it. Television producers and comic-book publishers know it
right well. But it took the dydee processors to scale, psychologically speaking, Everest. And there they stand, waving white
flags that have nothing to do with surrender.

AT THE SUMMIT

The Gifted Child

"The increased interest in the gifted, which is being awakened in the professions, in art, government, industry and labor, affords one of the greatest opportunities to safeguard our present world leadership against destructive ideologies which threaten democracy."
—Pauline Brooks Williamson, Executive Secretary, The American Association for Gifted Children

In 1957 Sputnik and the gifted child, in that precise order, attained a spectacular ascendancy. Sputnik has since come down, but the gifted child has if anything soared even higher, and now flies with the gods. It was in the wake of that first satellite that Washingtonians of substance made known that America's most precious product was her gifted children—

especially her scientifically gifted children—and that what was needed to make the world and space safe for democracy was more and better budding Norbert Wieners.

Thus it was that the tot with the high I.Q. became the child of the hour. Almost any child, as we have seen, can be a powerful status symbol. But some children make better symbols than others. The well-adjusted child is near the top of the hierarchy, although his status is waning. Then there are such *rarae aves*, and hence all the more exclusive symbols, as the only child (the breed is getting rarer every day), and the adopted child—right up there, particularly when he turns out well. But the true elite is the gifted child. For competitive parents he is the apotheosis of status symbols, and any parent who finds one about the house is clearly, in the current climate, holding the winning sweepstakes ticket.

By the present line of thinking all children deserve the very best except the gifted, who deserve even better. This is in marked contrast to the pre-Sputnikian philosophy, wherein it was widely held that the gifted child, being gifted, would pretty well muddle through on his own. Such inquiries as were made into his nature and nurture—most notably, the monumental Terman studies—were very scholarly affairs, known only in professional circles. Beyond the pilot programs in a few communities, there was little interest in creating special classes for the gifted. And there was only one official watchdog, The American Association for Gifted Children, whose spokesmen now take pride in noting that they were organized in 1946, long before the boom began, "when there were more people on the platform than in the audience." That, they say, took vision.

By contrast there are today, among others, a National Association for Gifted Children, a Council for the Education of the Gifted, and the Association of the Gifted ("Jumped on the bandwagon, all of them," says an American Association lady, a trifle surlily), and the house is packed at meeting-time. Books about the gifted spill over one another; women's magazines are studded with articles called "You and Your Gifted Child," and the P.T.A.'s devotion to the subject is supreme. Increasingly, the public schools make special provision for the gifted, either through segregated classes, some form of acceleration, or "enrichment," which Martin Mayer, in his book *The Schools*, has defined as "the intrusion into the classroom of prestigious middle-class interests"; and where the Board of Education doesn't act, the citizenry is pounding on the door. Controversies rage as to what kind of schooling is best for the gifted; the "heterogeneous group" people and the "homogeneous group" people hardly talk to each other any more. Washington's interest in the subject is sustaining, although some champions of the gifted child claim that it is not nearly strong enough. "Kennedy has allocated *so much* money for the mentally retarded," says one. "Of course, they need it too. But I just don't think it's fair that they get so much more than *our* children do." The prevailing spirit in this sense is not unlike that of, say, the American Cancer Society versus the March of Dimes. In short there is, as *The New York Times* soberly noted in a "Parent and Child" column, a "mania for creativity" awash in the land, and the child who has it is everybody's darling. The country loves him, the schools love him and oh, Lawdy, Lawdy, how the child worshipers love him.

The only trouble is that nobody knows exactly who he is. There are myriad definitions, some of which seem aimed at increasing the supply of gifted children by downgrading the requisites. By some standards—say, the top one per cent in intellectual ability at I.Q. 150 and up—the gifted are a very exclusive group. By others the estimates range as high as nine million children; three million is generally considered a nice conservative figure by the liberals and a nice liberal figure by the conservatives. Some school administrators play it straight: Any child with an I.Q. of 130 or better may be considered gifted. However, there is a widespread professional dissatisfaction with the practice of gauging giftedness by I.Q. alone. An educator suggests the definition: "Any child is potentially 'gifted' whose performance in a valuable line of human activity is consistently remarkable." But who is to say what is a valuable line of human activity?

Then there are a number of experts who have come up with five-point plans for identifying giftedness. One such: "(1) The gifted child is curious—always asking Why. (2) He wants to read and tries long before his time. (3) He is a nonconformist—won't take pat answers. (4) He has a bent in a particular line—music or science or whatever. (5) He is physically well developed." Another five-point system, this one authored by pediatrician Milton Senn, gives the questing parent a better break. "Such children are quick to learn and are clever in figuring things out for themselves. They have excellent memories. They are likely to have several absorbing hobbies. They are not necessarily well coordinated. . . . May or may not be artistic . . ." An American Association lady, a poetess at heart, says, "The gifted child is one who sees things that others do not see." And finally, pointing to the farthest reaches of the national giftedness fever, comes this charitable view from a piece in the *Farm Journal* titled, "Your Child *Is* Gifted": "No school would ever call her gifted, but fortunately her mother feels that she is. She is a little below average. But she works to get her grades. *Perseverance* is her rare and valuable gift. . . ."

With such a whoop-de-do, it becomes clear that in some circles an average child is something of an embarrassment. Parents who are not in the height of fashion may still prefer a simple all-American boy, well adjusted to his peers. But for the true child worshiper, to have an average child is to be social small beer; to have a gifted child, on the other hand, is not only fashionable, not only desirable, but downright patriotic, rather like having an astronaut in the family. Competitive parents who have an undeniably exceptional child score an effortless coup. As for the others, they have taken to casting about frantically for some hint, however modest, of giftedness in their own back yards. Perhaps he is gifted, this seemingly bourgeois offspring, by some criterion as yet unknown; at worst, perhaps he is repressed, suppressed, underachieving so that his essential giftedness isn't showing through. And so they plow through the definitions, muttering, "There must be a gifted child in here *somewhere.*"

The anxiety engendered in such treasure hunts is fierce. At a testing center where the young are brought to establish their I.Q.'s, a psychologist says: "It's interesting to watch how the mothers sit outside my office while I'm testing the kids. You might think it was a hospital waiting room.

"I generally have a conference with the parent right after the test. The purpose is to get her to accept that child *whether he is gifted or not* [italics the author's]. If he has tested average, I have to be very gentle."

In fact, the crucial question no longer is simply whether or not a child is gifted, but *how* gifted. The kingpins belong in the "ninety-ninth percentile," a holy state which now has become part of the operative jargon, like "traumatic" and "relates well," but timelier. An I.Q. tester reports, "One woman came to me and said, 'I can't understand it. All my friends' children are in the ninety-ninth percentile. What's the matter with *mine?*' I told her, 'How do *you* know their children are all in the ninety-ninth? Would *you* tell *them* that *your* child wasn't?' That made her feel better. She said she had never thought of it that way before." Similarly, at Hunter Elementary School in New York, a mecca for many mothers because it enrolls only gifted tots and because it is free, a spokesman says, "We haven't met a mother yet whose child isn't in the ninety-ninth percentile. Makes you wonder where all the other kiddies went to." And a lady among whose intimates I.Q. testing is now very much the thing says, "In my group there is only one parent who says her child isn't in the ninety-ninth. She goes around telling people he tested out in the eighty-eighth. Everyone thinks she is some kind of a nut."

"It seems to me," says a clinical and research psychologist who has been poking, officially, into the clockworks of gifted children and their parents, "that there are fads in parental pressures. Ten years ago the competition centered on who had the best-adjusted child. Today the competition is in terms of I.Q. and achievement. Mothers used to say, 'Why does my boy study all the time? Why doesn't he play baseball?' Now it's the other way around. There is this enormous pressure on the bright child to succeed brilliantly, and soon he starts pressuring himself. I have a patient, an eleven-year-old boy in an advanced class in school, who said to me, 'If I'm *really* of superior intelligence, how come other guys get better marks?' The boy has 135 I.Q. and performs very well. Unfortunately there are kids in the class who have 140 I.Q. and perform even better, and it is eating him and his mother up alive."

The advanced-class system poses many such problems. In a central Connecticut community of solid citizens, an elementary school principal made bold to divide the classes into five groups, working downward from the brightest in Class One. Form letters were sent to all parents, informing each where her child stood in this pecking order. The letters went out in June, on the last day of school; the principal had a busy summer.

"The telephones started ringing the next day," she recalls, still aquiver. "Of course the loudest screaming came from the parents of the kids in Group Two. 'My child is just as smart as so-and-so's kid'—oh, God, how many times I heard *that*.

"It has gotten so bad that for many of our parents there is a stigma attached to having an average child. All of a sudden being average means being *below* average. When their kids don't get into the I.G. [intellectually gifted; in such circles the abbreviation is as explicit as "ninety-ninth"] classes they start worrying and looking for private schools. I get mothers in here asking if they should have their children tutored because the kids are only getting a B."

In New Jersey an elementary school teacher, working with advanced-section children, says: "You have to defend your right to give any of these kids less than an A. The parent comes in for a conference and says belligerently, 'What's the matter with my child that he didn't get an A?' What she means is, 'What's the matter with *you* that he didn't get an A?' It seems to me that the whole thing has been twisted and distorted. The kids come to me not in search of knowledge, but asking how they can get better marks. They are really asking, 'What kind of answers do you want from me so that you will give me an A?' " Gratuitously, she offers up a small sociological tidbit: "I used to work in Newark, in a working-class neighborhood. The parents' emphasis was on behavior. In this town [it is a suburb, solidly upper-middle] the emphasis is on producing. A very large proportion of these kids are *expected* by their parents to be gifted. The feeling is, if my child isn't up there, something is wrong with me, or with him, or with his teachers. But there is definitely *something* wrong."

In one large city the I.G. program begins in fourth grade. Children who score above 130 in I.Q. testing and get maturity clearance from staff psychologists are candidates for the program. At that point, the superintendent of schools explained recently, "We call in the parents of all these prospective I.G. pupils. We give them a true picture of the program and the hard work. We tell them of the sacrifices their children will have to make—no more dancing lessons, no music lessons, no art or dramatic lessons, and so forth. Most of them are willing to make the sacrifice."

Seven mothers of these sacrificial lambs then were asked, individually, for their opinions of the program. Six turned thumbs down, each noting that the course of study was not advanced enough for her child. ("Why, my sister's son gets more enrichment where he goes to school," one said, "and he is *not even gifted!*")

Opinions rendered, a lady on the Board of Education was approached for a few dispassionate facts, and reported briskly: "My daughter is too bright for the program. She is a candidate in the second grade, and I can already tell. In school she is reading primers but at home she is reading fourth- and fifth-grade books. I went to the library and found a wonderful series of books, just perfect for these children. My daughter loved them. So I brought one into the school and said to the teacher, 'Why aren't you using this book?' And she said, 'Well, I didn't know anything about it.' So I said, 'Well, you do now. Now, you go right out and buy it.' That's the *only* way to get things done." The Board of Education is a nifty place for mothers of the gifted.

At a well-known testing center, there is a good gray-haired lady who tests pre-nursery-schoolers for entrance to the strongholds of the gifted, as well as for their parents' own edification, and who probably knows as much about the traumatic implications therein as anyone else in the country. For mothers who travel in the testing circuit she is something of a legend and a landmark; some swear by her, others at her. "If the child tests high," she says, regarding her schizophrenic image with calm, "everything is wonderful, including me. If he doesn't I am no good, or the child wasn't feeling well, or the test was done in too great a hurry. I've heard that last one so often that I now have developed a nice trick: If I finish with the child in half an hour, I keep him in my office for an extra fifteen minutes, just talking about little nothings, before I send him back out to his mama.

"Very often, if a child tests high enough to be accepted by a school for the gifted, the mother asks me, 'Does going to this kind of school develop snobbishness in children?' I tell her, 'No, but it can in parents.' I tell mothers that if the child does get a little cocky they should compensate by saying to him, 'Look, Johnny, you go to a gifted school and Joey doesn't, but remember that Joey plays the piano better than you do.' " (Whether many mothers take this advice, she doesn't know. The chances are as good that they will want to know why Johnny, being gifted and all, can't play the piano at least as well as Joey.) "They often have their children coached for the test. They deny it when I ask them but I can always tell, and I put it into the report to the school. Of course, that almost automatically screens out the child."

This is bad news for many. To the uninitiated, the spectacle of three-year-olds being primed for their confrontation with Stanford-Binet is bizarre, but the practice is prevalent enough. In some areas professional coaching of the preschool set has become a sort of educational specialty, wherein private tutors do better than eke out a living. Morality aside, the lures of the coaching system are understandable. Schools that enroll only gifted children are exceedingly few; and while the private schools, as we have seen, have a variety of social snobberies, the schools for the gifted are snobbish about one thing only:

intellectual capacity. With competitive fires raging as high as they do nowadays, most of the privates do have a disproportionate number of extremely bright moppets. But still, they have to make room for the offspring and siblings of alumni, who aren't necessarily brainy at all; and, as noted earlier, many of them are concerned with maintaining a "balanced student body," a democratic amenity that the gifted-school people don't give a hoot about. The latter are concerned, to some degree, about the "social maturity" of their applicants; the boom for brainpower has not yet gone so far that schools for the gifted are putting out welcome mats for maladjusted geniuses. But the healthiest psyche in the world doesn't stand a chance in one of these schools unless an impressive I.Q. goes along with it.

This only increases the prestige and desirability of such schools. "If your child gets into a good private school," says a mother who is intimately acquainted with the protocol, "everyone knows you have money or social position or a very capable child. If he gets into a gifted school, everyone knows you have a healthy genius. That is much better."

Thus, while waiting lines form outside the doors of all the better privates, at schools for the gifted they wind several times around the block. Hunter, in New York, is a prime example. Hunter's entrance requirement is 130 I.Q., plus reasonable evidence of social maturity; in a recent season there were 2,000 applications for 22 available places in the nursery school, and the lowest I.Q. admitted was 158. (It was at Hunter that a visitor, making the rounds of several classrooms, was told by a teacher, "We really should see that the children have clean fingernails. But after all, they *are* gifted.")

"The kids are geniuses," one mother says. "They go around, these little people, saying, 'My I.Q. is 160—what's yours?' Shakes you up a bit when you hear them. I wanted terribly to get my daughter in. When she was rejected I was crushed. I wondered what was wrong with her. I thought I'd failed. My husband had quite a time calming me down. I mean, he had to keep reminding me that her I.Q. was 141 and what the hell, that's not exactly *retarded*. It was just that anyone rejecting my child made me feel funny, that's all." There is a locally well-known case of one parent, level-headed soul, who got her daughter into the school and then pulled her out again. "When she started running around telling everyone, 'I'm an exceptional child,' my husband and I decided it simply wasn't the place for her." But it is just one case.

The procedure of getting into one of the gifted-child schools reduces the private school application ritual, including even the rigors of the Interview, to an almost benign experience. A fairly typical description is given by one woman who has a son at Hunter. The report is made a year after the event, but the lady remembers details as though these were war memoirs—which, in a sense, they are:

"I filed an application on February first at nine A.M. I was the first in line. As a matter of fact I was one of the first in the city to call for an appointment for testing.

"We got the appointment for two weeks later at the New York University Testing Center. On that day Eric was sick. I called the center and asked if we could come the next week instead. The woman laughed and said, 'Oh, my goodness, no! We are booked solid till April.' So April came, April fourteenth it was, and down we went. I didn't want to tire Eric with the test coming up, so we took a cab downtown. The psychologist was too busy to see me after the test. Eric wouldn't tell me anything about it, but it was a very positive experience for him, I could tell. We took a bus home.

"I spent nearly five *horrible* weeks just waiting. Finally, on

May fourteenth, we got a letter from the testing center saying that Eric was in the ninety-ninth percentile. It was a great relief. I was dying to know his I.Q. but the only way I could get it was by releasing the score to my pediatrician, and I didn't want to do that. I mean, he is a good pediatrician and all, but he has a big mouth and he takes care of all my friends' children and I didn't want him going into their homes and blabbing about my child's I.Q.

"Another six weeks went by before we were told to come to Hunter for the interview. It was a group interview. Positively nerve-wracking. The interviewer flung questions at the mothers like, 'Now, then, Mrs. X, when did you discover *your* child was intellectually gifted?' We just weren't prepared for it. Some of the mothers said their children seemed to be well coordinated at an early age, or toilet-trained early—things like that. I told him I had known Eric was gifted when he was eighteen months old because he was talking just as he talks today. [Eric is four.]

"Eric is very happy at Hunter. I knew he would make it. I applied because everyone in our socioeconomic [her very words] group does it, and because what have you got to lose? Just fifteen dollars for the application. Some of these mothers think their children are real geniuses and *must* go to Hunter. I don't consider Eric a genius—simply a very, very gifted child, and I am glad that he is among his peers. He would have been miserable in a public school with average children."

Not all Hunter mothers are similarly contented. Many express a curious dissatisfaction with the prize they toiled so hard to win. One says, "The staff wants to run the school its own way, that's the trouble. They have a very negative attitude about parents. When you ask why the second-graders can't go to school past noontime, they say, 'There is plenty *you* can do

to enrich your child's life when he is home. You can take him
to museums and concerts.' All that business. They seem to
imply that I want to spend less time with my child. It's not
that at all. I simply want her to *learn more.*"

Other parents complain that the school is used too much as
a teacher-training program for students at the Hunter School
of Education. "Actually," one says, "I think a child can get a
better education at one of the good private schools. But even
parents who can afford to send their kids to the most expensive
privates try to get them into Hunter instead." Why so? "Why,
because *everybody knows it is for gifted children.*"

The principal, Louie T. Camp, a sprightly young man
rather on the order of actor Eddie Albert, takes the com-
plainants in stride, as he can well afford to. "I think in actual
fact most of the mothers who knock the school are those
whose children didn't make it. With the competition we've
got, a kid of 135 I.Q. doesn't stand a chance. If the mothers
are disappointed it is understandable. They are rejected
mothers. . . ."

"A Hunter mother," a reverse snob has said, "treats everything her child says as a communication. And she wonders
how all the other kids ever got into the place."

It is true that parental competition tends to be particularly
dense wherever the gifted gather. Mothers of the gifted tots at
one school, especially the nursery set, like to spend a lot of
time on the premises, giving moral support to their own offspring and warily eying the competition. "I look around at
some of these kids," one says, "and they don't look so gifted
to me. There is one who is absolutely brilliant, I don't deny it,
but socially he is two years old. This boy's parents are the kind
who buy a new car and don't take off the price tag till they get
it home for his approval. One rainy day I offered the mother a

ride home and she said, 'Wait, I'll go ask Lewis if I can leave now'—and Lewis said no. My child is four months younger and *much* more mature."

Another says of a schoolmate who was invited to her daughter's birthday party, "I had always thought she was such a nice, gifted little girl, but at our house I realized she was a brat. I took the children to the store and she had a fit because I wouldn't buy anything for her. You call *that* gifted?"

But more often mothers of the gifted, themselves generally a brainy breed much given to lamenting the child-centeredness of our culture, play it with becoming modesty: "He's just a nice clever little boy, that's all. At the school they tell me he's a near-genius, but I don't believe it for a minute." Another, told how especially bright and appealing her best friend's child, also gifted, seems to be: "You really think so? I do adore him, but he's always seemed a lit-tle babyish to me." And: "Believe me, I envy women who have average children. My husband and I just can't keep up with this child."

This last is a common, albeit enviable, dilemma. Like pop art, the gifted child may be prestigious to own but a mighty strain to live with. Thus the mother of a gifted eight-year-old reports, with a warm mixture of pride and apology, the following conversation:

DAUGHTER: The teacher was very startled today. I think it was because I answered a question without raising my hand.

MOTHER: What was the question?

DAUGHTER (poker-faced): Well, the teacher said, "Here is a sentence: 'Timmie ain't going to the circus today.' What is the word we should never use?" And I said, "Shit! That is the word we should never use."

(It was a progressive school and all was forgiven. "Forgiven!" commented an educator to whom the story was repeated. "I know of some schools where they would have made the child valedictorian of her class.")

Mothers of the gifted—some refer to themselves as "gifted mothers," purely a semantic convenience—are strikingly well informed about intellectual giftedness. Many of them know the research. They speak with authority of "first-order" and "second-order" giftedness, of "enrichment," "advanced placement," "homogeneous grouping." They know to a woman that the stereotype of the brainy child as a ninety-pound weakling with bifocals is long since disproven—"Terman's research, you know." And they particularly like the research which has shown—although there is still some argument among the experts—that gifted children are plagued by no more neuroses than anybody else. This is a sensitive point for the gifted mother. One says, typically: "He may be brilliant, but otherwise he is *just* a normal, happy, outgoing little boy, exactly like all the others."

"We assure our parents that they don't have to worry about the emotional development of their children," says Dr. Benjamin Fine, headmaster of the Sands Point Country Day School for gifted children and onetime education editor of *The New York Times.* "We are concerned with the mental, physical, social and emotional adjustment of the child. These are my four planks."

Housed in the fading glory of a Gatsby-like estate on Long Island, New York, Sands Point is in its fourth season as a school for gifted children, after having been merely a school for eleven years. The average public school I.Q. spread is 90-140; in Sands Point it is 130-190—"although," as headmaster Fine points out, "the child with 130 seems rather slow here." Unlike Hunter, the school is private, and the tuition steep: $1,500 in the lower grades, $1,800 in the upper, including hot lunches. This doesn't stop parents, one of whom put the family budget back in balance by cutting out summer camp for her prodigy. ("No sacrifice is too much," she says.) There are hundreds of applicants on the scholarship wait list alone. Following an efficacious exposure on a Chet Huntley television show last winter ("The Pursuit of Excellence: Educating the Gifted Child"), it became necessary to install extra telephone lines to handle all the inquiries. Since it is not a live-in school, pupils must make their homes in the area. This doesn't stop parents either: a number of out-of-state families, including one that dwelt on the shores of the Pacific, have sold homes, changed jobs, and arrived bag and baggage to deliver their young to whatever muses prevail at Sands Point.

Sitting in his office, Dr. Fine ponders why it is that so many are so willing to give up so much. "We are now the brain center of the country," he says. "We are ideal because we are segregated. The segregation of brains is the best kind of segregation there is."

A mother, twice-blessed in the possession of two gifted children at the school, nods earnestly. "The wisest thing I ever heard," she says, "goes like this: 'There is nothing as unequal as the equal treatment of unequals.' Doesn't that really *say* it?

"Public schools were a nightmare for my children, I can tell you."

What was their problem? she is asked.

"Oh, it wasn't *their* problem. My children are happy, charming, good-looking, very well adjusted. It was the *schools'* problem." And overcoming what is, as she says, a natural reluctance to talk too much about her children, this Sands Point mother speaks:

"At one and a half Ted had a repertoire of sixty nursery rhymes which he would recite at the drop of a hat to anyone who asked him. I believe at four months he was saying Mama. He was drawing figures at two and a half, and discovered by himself how to multiply at four. His I.Q. was given as 150. I believe it is higher.

"Susan, my other child, has 165 I.Q. That means she is one in ten thousand. I read her report some time ago, through dubious means—I persuaded a nursery school teacher. I just *had* to know.

"What makes my children stand out even here at Sands Point is that they retain so well—isn't that so, Dr. Fine?" The headmaster nods emphatically, but clearly is engrossed in desk papers. The lady waits a moment to recapture his attention, doesn't, and continues to an audience of one: "My husband's I.Q. is 152. I am a Phi Bete. I consider myself bright, but I don't know if I'm way up there. My father is most unusual. He almost had a great novel published. They never could measure his I.Q., it was so high. My husband's father is brilliant. And *his* father was a philosopher, a profound man.

"I put Ted into public nursery school. Very soon he came home and said, 'Why don't I learn? I don't want to play, I want to learn.' It was pathetic. I had him tested and had the report sent to the principal. And you know what he said when I told him I wanted Ted accelerated? He said, 'Why don't you take him to baseball games?'

"But the first-grade teacher was thrilled with him. She said he would be the future great scientist of America, so I knew she was sympathetic and asked her to give him more arithmetic. The principal got mad and transferred him to another heterogeneous group.

"I might say in passing that the worst place to get anything done for gifted children is in the upper-middle-class suburb, where all the children are going to go to college and all the parents want equality—'democratic education' for all. [In the sense that nobody fights harder for the gifted than the parents of the upper-middle-class community, this is a curious view; in the sense that so many want to join the fight, the lady has a point.] If they give one child advantages the other mothers yell. That's what was so horrible.

"When I took my children out of public school, the mothers were very spiteful. They would talk to me about everything except my children. Basically they are very jealous. You know, they *all* think they have exceptional children, and they are resentful of me. Naturally, with such children, I am very selective of my friends.

"My children are here to get the best education possible, which they deserve. Getting a child into Sands Point is something. And *two* children—well, that is very, very rare." (Not so, a helpful secretary comments: There are about a dozen families with two children in the school, and even one family with three. Three! The lady is perturbed. "But," she says, "they're not *all three* over 150 I.Q., are they?")

Approaching the children's dining room: "Ted doesn't know yet whether he wants to be an archaeologist, a scientist, a writer, or an artist. Once I heard him and his buddies talking about what they would do if they were President, and one of the boys said, 'Aw, who wants to be President!' But Ted was able to recognize the possibility, to discuss it sensibly and talk about what he would do. He is now reading *The Making of the President*. He loves to read. I have never made him feel he had to go out and play rather than read."

And there, in the dining room, stands Ted. "What are you doing?" asks his mother. "Playing," says Ted, and runs away.

Seated at the staff table, she looks up, sees a teacher approaching, and waves her over. "Come join us!" she says. "You know, I never go on and on like this about the children, but I would like you to hear what I was saying before. It is very interesting.

"At one and a half Ted had a repertoire of sixty nursery rhymes which he would recite at the drop of a hat to anyone who asked him. I believe at four months . . ."

"It is true," the headmaster says later, "that some parents of the gifted are exploiting them. They wear their children's achievements on their lapels. You get a five-year-old doing second-grade work and his mother wants him working faster. She wants to be able to say, 'My child is brilliant. He is five years old and doing eighth-grade work.' But most of our parents are here because they don't know what to do with these children."

This is a two-way street. Often, the gifted child doesn't know what to do with his parents, either. Says psychologist Boris M. Levinson in a report on the gifted:

"He is like the goose that lays the golden eggs. Immediately the parents think and feel about social advancement for themselves, sometimes forgetting about their child in the process. They can lord it over their friends and neighbors. . . . The child is thus 'enslaved' with the responsibility of providing the family with 'prestige.' His accomplishments are no longer his —they are his parents' and he is left alone, his accomplishments exposed to the winds of envy which he feels directed towards him from every quarter."

But the *really* gifted child has recourse: he can become a failure. Levinson has chronicled the case of a boy, David, who was tested at five and found to have an I.Q. of 175. The teacher explained to his family that this was a very significant I.Q., being in the genius category. The information was conveyed posthaste to relatives, neighbors, and to the child himself. Says Levinson: "Everything at home became subordinate to his interests, ambitions, and needs. At the age of six he received an *Encyclopædia Britannica* from his aunt which was inscribed 'To our little genius. Some day we will read about your exploits in books such as these.' " David was feeling no pain. He began dropping the friends who weren't good enough for him to play with, and made life hard for those who remained. He was taken out of his class and sent to an exclusive private school, whereupon his troubles began: Nobody liked him.

This trend rose steadily throughout his early school career. By the time David was ready for college he was so thoroughly unlovable that not even the Ivy League colleges wanted him, although he was a genius. He finally made it into a tough non-Ivy school—as a science major, of course—where he began getting B and C grades and eventually achieved the unspeakable: a D in chemistry. He decided he didn't like science, which severely shook his parents. He switched schools and began majoring in music, wherein, when last heard from, he was uninspired in original composition but showing a nice knack for rearranging.

"This change of career," reports Levinson, "has brought about a crisis in David's family relationships. His father threatened to disown him, since when he entered college all the family friends were advised that David was studying medicine and the father was already seeking an office for his son, the future doctor and maybe psychiatrist. The mother is crestfallen. She cries all night. She is ashamed to meet her former cronies at bridge parties. She has dropped out of the P.T.A. . . . She does not even attend open-school week, as she is ashamed to face the teachers who always inquire as to how David, the genius, is making out."

In Dr. Levinson's view David and his dispirited folk, though

they are extreme, point a moral. "I don't believe in 'intellectually gifted children,' " he says, casually committing a heresy.
"We can raise the I.Q.'s of most of our citizenry enormously.
I see the gifted child as a little freak. Most of the ones we see
are actually kids who come from privileged backgrounds. They
are middle-class, and the I.Q. tests are geared to the middle
class, and so they make a splendid showing." (A New York
University tester has commented: "We find that very bright
children generally have bright and economically well-off parents—but we don't like to admit it.")

"We create special categories to get special monies. When
a need arises you have to philosophize great theories to structure it. So we make big theories and small categories: the
gifted child, the retarded child, the mentally ill child. Soon
we will be like *Brave New World,* with the Alpha, Beta and
Gamma people.

"It is not inherent in the nature of the gifted child that he
has to be in a separate class. From the educational and psychological points of view, there is no justification for it. It
creates invidious social distinctions. But people want it. Why?
Because they want an elite, and right now the intellectual elite
happens to be the most stylish. We are substituting an aristocracy of brains for an aristocracy of wealth or birth.

"I would like to see the child we call 'gifted' in a class with
children his own age, all kinds of children, where each would
work at his own pace and we would help each to develop to
his fullest capacity. The answer is not to segregate them, but
to challenge them. The child who is exposed to stimulating
work will *work.* But listen, who listens to me? The way things
are going right now, ideas like mine are not too popular."

They are popular enough with a lot of experts. With a lot
of other experts—gifted-school-type experts, gifted-organiza-

tion-type experts, and many, many gifted-parent-type experts—they are odious, and show a total insensitivity to the special nature and needs of the gifted child. To the special needs, in fact, of all exceptional children—the slow ones as well as the brightest. And somewhere, beyond and slightly above it all, hovers a suspicion that the average child, sweet anachronism, is getting lost in the shuffle.

"We once had a meeting at which a governor kept talking about how important the 'in-betweens' are," says a member of the American Association for Gifted Children. "And I thought, Lord, if he doesn't shut up about those in-betweens and start talking about the gifted fast, he'll hear about it before he gets off the platform. Our ultimate goal, of course, is to help *all* children—and we believe by helping the gifted we are helping all children." How, she doesn't say.

Another champion of the elite says, "Unfortunately, there are still far too many schools that are more interested in the average and the retarded child . . ."—and makes them sound almost synonymous.

"It is a great mistake that during these years we have cut back on research on the average child," says Hunter's Principal Camp, more charitable than many who occupy such strongholds as his. And a public school principal mourns: "All our P.T.A. wants to talk about is special programs for the gifted. How about the child in the middle? I put it to them once that he was being neglected, and they all agreed it was a shame, and then went right back to talking about the gifted."

"There is a great danger," Martin Mayer has written, "that the current 'quest for excellence' will turn into an emphasis on the education of the easily educable. . . . A decade ago, the line of least resistance for the schools was to organize a program so easy that nobody could get mad at the superintendent because his child was flunking. Today, the line of least resistance is to work only with children who don't need much work. . . ."

Poor, passé, average child. Everyone wants a wee giftee. And yet there are not—not by any definition—enough to go around. What is to be done?

Fortunately there are other ways to reap status from a child —even an average child. We have examined some of them in the preceding pages. True child worshipers will find still others, and they will come through however high the handicap— which is to say, however low the I.Q.

And for child worship itself, the future looks grand. Today it is an American phenomenon; tomorrow, who knows? "Freedom of the individual," says psychiatrist Lena Levine, "is so much the core of our country. The parents have it, and so the children want it too. That is our democratic family system; it was born here, and worked through here, and it will spread. In this regard we are a laboratory for the world. We lead the way. Europeans and Asians still have the patriarchal system. They still like children in their place, but it won't last. They will come to our point of view. The democratic family is already a reality in some parts of Europe, and it will come into being everywhere. It is the family of the future."

Thus, a new day dawning.

ACKNOWLEDGMENTS

Some time back this writer did an article for *The New York Times Magazine* titled "Three-Year-Olds in $200 Dresses," intended as a lighthearted report on high style among the pre-pubescents. In the course of research, a child psychiatrist was asked why some mothers kept their young looking so chic; could it be that they were using their children as status symbols? He answered the question with a question, as psychiatrists so often do: "Do mothers ever *not* use their children as status symbols?"

This seemed too provocative a notion not to pursue, and the farther it was pursued the more provocative it became. Pursued? It was a tiger caught by the tail. It led first, with the writer merely hanging on, to a revelation of the countless ways in which parents do use their children; and ultimately,

· 247 ·

three years and much research later, to this report on the national climate of child worship.

Is that climate good or bad? Reporters do not belong on the editorial page, and considerable effort has been made here to leave editorializing to the specialists. Just as considerable effort has been made to stress the fact that everyone is not a child worshiper. If the shoe fits, fair enough; but there has been no attempt to slip it onto any reluctant foot. The material virtually dictated its own shape. The child worshipers were plentiful, and throughout these pages they have been speaking for themselves.

Throughout these pages, too, a good many other people have been speaking whose relationship to child worship is professional rather than personal. Each has observed it within his special sphere, which is to say within each of the areas covered in this book, and I should like to cite some—of many—who have spoken with particular authority, concern, and helpfulness.

Among those who have given general testimony on the child-centered life: Margaret Mead, who pointed the way toward several rich research lodes; Marya Mannes and Harvard's Florence Kluckhohn, both eloquent on the subject of the Good or Professional Mother; John W. M. Whiting, also of Harvard, David Sills of Columbia, and a large number of psychiatrists, psychoanalysts, and psychologists through whose offices legions of child worshipers have marched—most notably, Lena Levine, Allan Fromme, Nathan Ackerman and Francis Bauer.

Among the specialists viewing the child-centered house: Ada Louise Huxtable, architectural critic for *The New York Times;* architect Edward D. Stone, who spoke feelingly and from the shoulder; architects Herman York and Stanley Shaftel, also fervent, and many home builders; Cynthia Kellogg, decorating editor for the *Ladies' Home Journal,* and Elizabeth Sverbeyef of *The Times;* home decorators from leading department stores in several metropolises, including Boston, Philadelphia, Washington, and Chicago, who viewed all those antique cribs and private telephones with whimsy, and interior designers from a number of smart New York decorating firms, who viewed not with whimsy but were helpful nonetheless.

Specialists on the P.T.A. and the schools—public, private and For Gifted Only: Martin Mayer, whose book *The Schools* was an education in itself; Boris Levinson of Yeshiva University Psychological Center; Fred Hechinger, education editor of *The New York Times;* Elizabeth Wrenn of the West Hartford, Connecticut, school system; Benjamin Fine of the Sands Point Country Day School, Louie T. Camp of Hunter Elementary School, and spokesmen for the American Association for Gifted Children; the teaching and administrative staffs of many private schools, including Loomis, Collegiate, Chapin, Dalton, Horace Mann, Lenox, Brearley, and Miss Porter's of Farmington, Connecticut, whose fame, whatever time may bring, rests immortal in Jacqueline Kennedy; officials of, among other public school systems, those in New York, New Haven, Hartford, Cleveland, Chicago, Miami, and Levittown, New Jersey; and P.T.A. presidents and members, past and present, from more cities than the author can remember, witnessed in action at more meetings than she can forget.

Specialists on parent education: Officials of the Child Study Association, the League for Parent Education, and Children's Services of Connecticut; the U.S. Children's Bureau; Orville G. Brim, Jr., of The Russell Sage Foundation; *Parents' Magazine;* Dorothy Barclay, former Parent and Child editor of *The New York Times,* and Martin Tolchin and Phyllis Ehrlich, both of *The Times;* star performers on the lecture circuit, who give their best lectures when guaranteed anonymity, and the Parents' Groups and Mothers' Clubs themselves—clubs galore, members galore.

Specialists on the pediatrician's dilemma: the men who are feeling the pinch. Dozens of them, all tired, all articulate, all understandably loath to be identified—with one happy exception: Benjamin McLane Spock, who was most helpful and hospitable and, being out of private practice, is reasonably safe from maternal ire.

On the rites of child worship in the wide commercial world: Eugene Gilbert of Gilbert Youth Research, a clear-eyed observer; account executives, publicists, and copywriters handling pertinent accounts, notably the talented technicians of Kellogg, Campbell, and Ideal Toy; executives of the Diaper Service Industry Association, and a large assortment of supermarket managers, toy buyers, package designers, and diaper-service owners, none of whom seem to lead an easy life.

The specialists on Scarsdale: half the folks in town, or so it seemed. Their children being occupied in a good many other pursuits, they had time to give the interviewer, and they gave it with good will and grace.

On modern-day camps: officials and affiliates of the American Camping Association and the Association of Private Camps, on whose verdant acres many enlightening hours were spent; Kenneth Webb of the Farm and Wilderness Camps; Francine Foley Wells of the School and Camp Information Service of *The New York Times,* and camping specialists from the Boy Scouts and the Y.M.C.A.

On family vacations: the omniscient A.A.A.; *Camping* and *My Baby* magazines; public-relations people of the Conrad Hilton empire, who gave their all; the Connecticut, New York, and Miami Chambers of Commerce; Paul Friedlander, travel editor of *The New York Times;* spokesmen for star hostelries in the Catskill constellation, and vacation personnel from baby-sitters to junior-division social directors—on land, on the sea, in the air.

Specialists on pint-sized fashion: *Women's Wear Daily;* Patricia Peterson and the fashion staff of *The New York Times;* of many designers, three—Helen Lee, John Weitz, and Lilly Daché—who were particularly helpful; the redoubtable overseers of Saks Fifth Avenue's Baby Boutique and Bergdorf Goodman's Talcum Powder Room; Amy Vanderbilt, who commented feelingly on the etiquette of dressing children for status, and Dr. Leon McKinney, who commented as feelingly on the results.

On the social and cultural pursuits of the young: innumerable guides, such as dancing-school teachers, art instructors, and birthday-party packagers led the way; the true experts, however, were the children, who are their own best social historians.

Special thanks to Lester Markel, Sunday editor of *The New York Times,* who generously permitted the author a leave of absence to work on this project while employed by *The Times;* to Arthur Fields of Crown, an altogether indispensable editor; to Willard Gaylin, who helped the book begin; to Jon and Judith Lear, a pair of peerless press agents; and, finally, most thankfully to and for my husband, Harold Lear, without whose patience, support, and high tolerance for hamburger dinners the writer, if not the book, would surely have been undone.